auth LEADERSHIP THAT LASTS

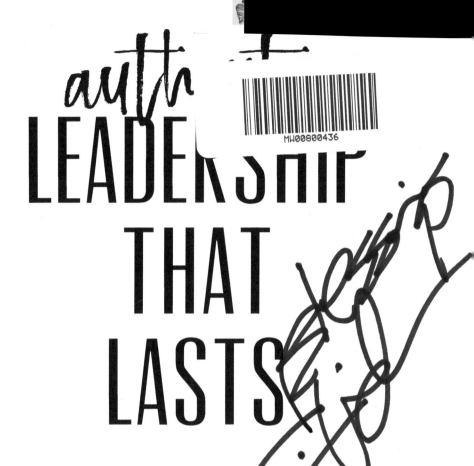

JIM WIDEMAN

A JIM WIDEMAN MINISTRIES, INC PUBLICATION
www.jimwideman.com

Jim Wideman Ministries, Inc
2441Q Old Fort Parkway #354
Murfreesboro, TN 37128

HELPING LEADERS THINK DIFFERENTLY AT HOME, AT CHURCH, AND IN EVERYDAY LIFE!

Authentic Leadership That Lasts: The You-Can-Do-It-Guide

Published by Jim Wideman Ministries, Inc
2441Q Old Fort Parkway #354
Murfreesboro, TN 37128

Printed in the United States of America

Visit our website **www.jimwideman.com**

Credits:
Editor: Joy Abad
Cover and Interior Design: Nicole Jones

ISBN 978-0-9838306-6-5 (Paperback)
ISBN 978-0-9838306-7-2 (ePub)

DEDICATION

Over thirty years ago, I began a journey that I'm still on today—a quest to move past "live well and do well" and to actually "lead well." After fifteen years on the job trying to do my best and working hard, I realized there was more needed than just hard work, or even smart work for that matter. I realized true authentic leadership doesn't come from a position or even a title; it comes from who you are, as well as, from who you are becoming. It comes from the inside out, and it is not a one-time choice; instead, it is the result of a daily choice to say yes to all of Jesus' invitations. I am so thankful that today as I am writing and making changes to a book that I published for the first time over twenty years ago, I am not the same person I was then. That's why this is not the same book. What a wonderful opportunity to have a second chance to add, to take away, and to make the changes that I've wanted to make as I have coached and taught through this material. I hope that wherever you are on your leadership journey that you'll listen to Holy Spirit and apply what He is speaking to you. We all have been called to be learners, and He is not done leading us and showing us what He wants us to know and become.

Once again, I'd like to dedicate this book to my fabulous family—my girls and also my grands! First, to my wonderful wife, Julie; thank you for helping me grow and make changes to become a better leader than I ever imagined I could be. Thanks for cleaning me up and pushing me forward. Thanks for never giving up on me and always loving me and supporting me! You are the best partner and helper a man could ever have.

And to our two girls, Yancy and Whitney, their husbands Cory and Nigel, and my three grandsons—Sparrow, Rhythm, and Royal: Thanks for allowing me to be a part of all of your worlds. You all are my bright spots. Thanks for making life fun and helping me to enjoy the trip. Thanks for teaching me so much. I am proud of you all and the choices you make. Thanks for how you love me and GG, for your families, and for the leaders each of you are! Thanks for allowing me the privilege to be your friend, as well as, your dad and your G. Each of you have made me a better person, father, and grandfather.

Also a big thank you to Team Jim—without them this book would not be possible.

To Corey and Nicole Jones for transcription, graphic design, and layout (plus late-night and early morning texts and calls). Also a huge thanks and shout-out to the one and only Joy Abad, my longtime editor. Thank you, team! You three mean the world to me. Thanks for always helping me with such excellence.

I would also like to dedicate this book to all the pastors and mentors that I have had the privilege of serving with and learning from over these last four-and-a-half decades and counting. Thank you, Pastor G.D. Wilson, for teaching me how to work; Pastor Dan Ronsisvalle, for teaching me to dream big; Pastor Cortez Fraizer, for teaching me to love God's people; Pastor Willie George, for teaching me how to pursue excellence and how to build a team; Pastor Allen Jackson, for teaching me to lead with integrity and to walk in forgiveness; and to Pastors Henry and Alex Seeley, who are showing me the importance of living and leading with the help of Holy Spirit. I am a better learner and a better leader because God put you in my life. Thanks a million!

TABLE OF CONTENTS

INTRODUCTION

Y ou can be a leader if you really want to be.

Some people think leadership is for a chosen few. I couldn't disagree more. The fact is that anyone can become a leader if that person really *wants* to be a leader and is willing to pay the price of leadership and servanthood.

Think about all of the people you know, and you'll be able to name a few folks who seem to just naturally—or supernaturally—have an abundance of the stuff leadership requires. They're organized. They're focused. They're able to gather people around a cause and get things done. You look at them and think, "Those people are born leaders."

And you're half right. They have been born, but they weren't born as leaders. The skills that make them leaders are skills they've learned along the way.

We're all born into this world naked and helpless. We can't do the first thing for ourselves. There was a time none of us knew how to do anything we can now do. There was a time we couldn't dress ourselves. We couldn't feed ourselves. We couldn't read this book. Now we've mastered those skills and many, many more. We can master the skills it takes to be a leader too. We can learn to be organized, to manage ourselves and others, to be an example worthy to be followed. They're all learned behaviors.

You see, leadership isn't about titles or paychecks or what's on your business card, resume, or your LinkedIn page. You don't have to be the head of a huge ministry to be a leader. If you're influencing others positively while doing what the Word says, and you are making a difference; you're a leader.

But not everyone is willing to do what it takes to be an authentic leader.

I'm a guitar player, and I've been playing a long time. But there are lots of guitar players in my church here in Nashville who put me to shame. They're far better, and there's a reason—they've paid a price I haven't been willing to pay. Whether you're mastering guitar chords or leading a ministry or running a business, it comes down to this—how badly do you want it? Are you willing to pay the price?

If the answer is *yes*, this book is for you. I've had the privilege of helping train thousands of people through conferences, consulting, and coaching; and I've yet to meet someone who absolutely, positively couldn't develop or sharpen their leadership skills. We can all get better at leading others—guaranteed.

But there's a big condition on that guarantee. Will you do what it takes? Are you willing to make changes in your life? Are you willing to make consistent changes and make consistent wise choices? Are you willing to live your life according to God's Word?

When I was in college, my major was *campus-ology*. That means that though I was at college; I wasn't really *in* college. I went to classes, but I was far more familiar with the places guitar players hung out to jam than I was familiar with the library. Being enrolled in college gave me the chance to have the time of my life.

But then Dr. Stanberry, one of my professors, pulled me aside and said, "Jim, you've got a lot of talent and ability, but you're one of the most disorganized people I've ever met. I want to help you."

I'd seen my grade-point average. I knew I needed help, so I agreed.

Here's what he did. He bought me a calendar—the first one I'd ever owned. He showed me how to write down what I was supposed to be doing. My class schedule went into the calendar and so did my assignments. We laid it all out in black and white.

But Dr. Stanberry knew I needed more. So we regularly met and worked on using that calendar to break my disorganized habits. I had to learn to be focused, and organizing my calendar led to organizing my life, which led to being able to organize my ministry.

That experience came back to me one day when I was reading 1 Corinthians 12:28. In this verse Paul lays out how we're all part of the body of Christ. We all have unique gifts and tasks and roles to fill: "And in the church God has appointed first of all apostles, second prophets, third teachers, then workers of miracles, also those having gifts of healing, those able to help others, those with gifts of administration, and those speaking in different kinds of tongues."

Look at that list. All those roles were appointed by the Lord. They were all sanctioned, all necessary. But look closely at the questions Paul asks in verses 29 and 30: "Are all apostles? Are all prophets? Are all teachers? Do all work miracles? Do all have gifts of healing? Do all speak in tongues? Do all interpret?" The obvious answer to each question is a resounding *no*. We're not all teachers, prophets, or apostles.

I must have read that passage ten million times before I noticed that two roles Paul mentioned in verse 28 aren't mentioned later. Those two roles are the ability to help others and the role of administration. Why didn't Paul list these? I don't think it's a stretch to conclude that everyone can participate in those ares of ministry. We all can be helpers. We all can be organized and provide oversight and leadership.

Think about it. Even very young children can be helpers. Even very young Christ followers can be helpers. We *all* can be helpers. And in the same way, no matter what our ministry is in the church—from the senior pastor to the people directing traffic out in the parking lot—there's got to be some administration and organization in what we're doing.

Administration, one of the cornerstones of capable leadership, is for everyone. And the administrative skills that will help you provide excellent leadership can be learned, honed, and sharpened.

It takes work. It takes intentionally. It isn't easy.

But the results will allow you to be more effective and fulfilled in ministry, as well as, in business and becoming the leader God knows you can be—that He designed you to be. As you add tools to your leadership tool belt, God will provide opportunities to use those new skills to bless others and to advance His kingdom.

Growing in your leadership abilities is an investment—one that will pay dividends for your entire life.

Ready to grow in your leadership? You *can* do it!!

CHAPTER 1:
LEADERSHIP FROM THE INSIDE OUT

If you're looking for an unlikely leader in ministry or in life, I'm your guy. When I think back to how I lived in high school, even I would have voted myself "least likely to succeed."

I wish I could blame someone except myself. My mother, a single mom raising two kids and supporting her own mother, did the best she could. I had a lot of friends, many of whom I'm still in touch with today. (Thanks, Facebook!) There were people in my life who cared about me. One of them, my best friend's dad, even got me a job playing guitar in his little bar band. I was making pretty good money for a kid. Of course, I was ten at the time. Looking back, that wasn't the smartest of decisions. One bad decision led to many bad decisions. How many? Well, to this day I don't remember my junior year in high school.

By the time the Lord got a hold of me and I headed off to Bible college, I was an old hippie, ex-dopehead, baby believer. The people at the church where I'd found Christ hadn't dared to tell me to shape up; they were just glad I wasn't dealing drugs. They waited until I was heading off to school to say, "You know, maybe it would help your ministry if you quit smoking."

But when I got to Bible college, some wonderful people helped me see what I could become, not in ten years but the next day. Small steps. Little steps.

And they didn't just help me remodel my outside; they focused on my inside. They helped me develop character. You see, in the kingdom of God, leadership isn't just about getting people to follow you. Anyone can do that. All you need is force.

Maybe you've seen those old westerns where the bad guys would storm into a bank, fire a couple of shots into the ceiling, and yell, "Everybody on the floor!" Those bank tellers dropped like bricks. As long as the bad guys had ammunition, they were in charge; people did what they said. But that's not a strategy I'd recommend for recruiting small-group leaders for the fourth and fifth graders in your ministry.

Leadership in ministry is all about encouraging others to reach the next level in their spiritual growth and choosing to develop your God-given skills. It's helping others develop. It's coaching and encouraging them to become all of what God wants them to become.

Ministry leaders influence people. They touch the lives of others. They impact others. They don't flash their job titles or their position around to make people fall in behind them. They don't even try to impress others with their accomplishments from the past or other seasons.

Authentic leaders, especially in ministry, grow from the inside out. Their leadership begins with their character. Someday when you're surfing the web, log on to Amazon or Apple Books, and browse every book they have listed on leadership. Mercy, it's a pretty long list!

Each year hundreds of books get published that describe leadership, dissect leadership, and write prescriptions for how to become a leader. Plus, there are countless vlogs, podcasts, master classes, workshops, and webinars. You could spend the next six months doing nothing but studying about leadership.

At the end of that time, you'd be well-informed but not necessarily a leader. Studying leadership principles and practices like the ones you'll find in this book are just a part of growing as a leader. And as much as any author hates to admit it about his or her book, it's probably the least important part.

If you just want to get your ministry in line, you can skip on ahead a couple of chapters and start doing all the things I describe. Those practical tools and tips will get your organization oiled up and running smoothly. And you'll look more like a leader than you've ever looked.

But if you want to be a leader—an authentic leader who's got what it takes to go the distance in serving God and the people around you—then get ready for some hard demanding work. And it starts not with your leadership techniques but with your heart and your willingness to respond to God's call to lead others. You have to be willing to consistently choose to be a doer of God's Word each and every day; to acknowledge that Father God gives you air to breathe every minute of every day; to take every thought captive and choose to align your thoughts with the Father's.

That's because being an authentic leader in ministry isn't measured by how many people are lined up behind you. It isn't measured by the size of your church or the number of players on your team. It's measured by whether you're pleasing Father God and doing what He wants you to do. I have worked on being a son of the Most High over the last few years, and it's affected the way I lead. Authentic leadership is born from a desire to be first and foremost a true son or daughter of the Most High God.

You will see your abilities grow because when you listen to God and do what He says, your choices will bring increase. God will bless what you put your hand to. That's how His kingdom works.

The starting place for us all is to desire to work on our intentionality to rely on Father God and learn how to be a son or a daughter who is listening to Holy Spirit and obeying fully what He's saying. Always stay teachable and willing to go where He's leading you, even if it's somewhere you've never gone before. We can trust our helper and our guide—Holy Spirit—to lead us in the ways we are to lead others.

THE NEED FOR AUTHENTIC LEADERSHIP

Now, I'm a southern boy, born and bred, and I've watched farmers work. Farmers find out right away that just because they put seeds in the ground it doesn't guarantee that plants will grow. If they want to see a harvest, they've got to tend to the seeds and make sure there's enough water, warmth, and fertilizer. If down the road anyone expects to pick crops, someone's got to be nurturing the young plants along the way.

And just like growth on a farm can't happen without a farmer, growth in the church can't happen without a leader. You won't see growth in your youth ministry, children's ministry, small groups, or anywhere else until someone says, "I'll take ownership and take charge of this. I'll do the things necessary to bring growth."

Leadership causes increase. When I look in the Bible, I see that it's God's will that growth happens in ministry. Jesus came to seek and to save those who are lost. We've been sent out to find those folks and bring them into community. The church is supposed to keep getting bigger.

Through the years, I've gotten criticized about being so concerned about tracking the numbers at every church I've been a part of. I've tried to know how many people come each week. I've tried to know how effectively we're reaching each age group. I've tried to know how much our budget is growing. I've tried to keep the numbers in front of me. Someone at every church has said, "All you care about are nickels and noses. You live in the book of Numbers, but you should live in the book of Acts."

Well, here's something I've learned throughout my leadership journey: *It takes nickels to reach noses.* If your budget doesn't grow, there will be ministry opportunities you can't pursue. If your services don't get more crowded, there are families you aren't reaching.

And don't confuse population shifts with true growth. When someone comes from another church to your church, that's not growth. That's population shift. Growth is addition. It means new salvations, new individuals and families, not individuals and families that wandered in from the church down the street.

Growth—real growth—is important.

Don't get me wrong. Having a small ministry isn't a bad thing. But if a ministry stays small, that can be a sign that something is wrong. And what's wrong is often a lack of proper leadership. As a rule, good leadership causes increase. Negative or poor leadership causes stagnation.

Throughout this book I'll share techniques with you that I've picked up from some of the best ministry leaders I know. I'll also tell you how I have led at past churches, as well as, what I am doing today to lead in this present season. No matter if you are new to this leadership way of life or if you've been on your leadership journey for years, it's all about being a person who's looking to learn and grow. I'm always looking to grow. I can learn something every day if I want to. And, believe me, I want to!

BEGIN AT THE BEGINNING

So get ready to receive some solid advice but not yet. First, let's talk about you.

People get into leadership roles for all sorts of reasons, sometimes for the wrong ones. I suspect if you're reading this book, you're in a ministry leadership role in your church, but are you an authentic leader? There's an easy way to find out the answer to that question. Look over your shoulder. Is anyone back there naturally following you? If not, you're not leading. You're just marching in a very short parade.

If you are leading others, whether it's one or one thousand, you've got to decide whether you're willing to do it Jesus' way. If so, you've got to be willing to be a servant because Jesus came to serve, not to be served. Here are three important targets to aim for to become a servant leader.

BE A SERVANT OF GOD

Serve the Lord in your deeds, not just in your words. I don't know about you, but I want to one day hear, "Well done, good and faithful servant." God doesn't hand out that welcome to just anyone who's had a ministry responsibility.

God reserves His praise for those who love Him, follow Him, and serve Him. What's important to Father is our hearts. We church leaders can't get so swelled up with self- importance that we forget to answer, "Yes, Lord," when Father asks us to do something. *We can't forsake our first love because we get distracted by doing ministry.*

Do people around you compliment you on how much you get accomplished or on how much your character reflects the character of God? Are you trusting, following, and serving God?

BE A SERVANT OF OTHERS

If you signed up so you could run the show or because you want to show people how a well-oiled machine is supposed to be run, you're in for a rude awakening. God just doesn't honor puffed-up leaders. He's funny that way. He isn't impressed with us. If His Son came here to serve and save, Father God figures we ought to be good for moving a few tables or listening to someone whose heart is broken.

Do people around you describe you as a servant of others? Why or why not?

BE A SERVANT OF THE TRUTH

If you're going to lead in ministry, you need a clear understanding of God's Word. What's the point of putting together a powerhouse organization if you don't have a purpose—fulfilling *God's* purpose for your ministry?

Is your heart in tune with God's heart for your ministry? Are you praying and listening to His voice? Are you growing in your relationship with God? Are you daily digging into His Word?

You can't lead people someplace you've never been or someplace you are not willing to go. If you want your ministry to grow deeper in the things of the Lord, go there yourself. Seek after Father's heart, and then invite others to follow along with you on the journey.

Ministry leadership—authentic ministry leadership—doesn't demand that we be perfect. But it does demand that we be people after God's own heart—from the inside out. We can't control what happens in life, but we can control how we respond. The right response comes from a heart after God. Ministry leadership is an overflow of our character.

Think about Moses. Now, I've never met the man, but I've thought a lot about him. I think if we had met Moses while he were still living in Pharaoh's household, we'd have recruited him onto our church executive team in a heartbeat. I suspect he looked and sounded like a leader—educated and trained in the court of a mighty king. He probably wore fine clothes and had the confident look of a man who was used to being taken seriously.

But he wasn't a leader fit to lead God's people. Not yet.

God had built all the right stuff into Moses. God knew He was going to call Moses into leadership. But I think before Moses could be used, he had to go tend sheep out in the wilderness with Jethro. Moses needed to grow in his understanding of his people's history and culture. Moses needed to learn to rely on God.

God didn't have Moses herd sheep for forty years to punish Moses. God used those years to prepare—to season and shape him—for leadership.

Like Moses, before we get too busy *doing* leadership, we've got to learn to follow God and let Him shape us into leaders—authentic leaders—from the inside out.

Are you ready for the ride? Let's go.

CHAPTER 2:
SEVEN TRAITS OF AUTHENTIC LEADERSHIP

Leadership is a double-edged sword. Leaders can use their influence for good . . . or evil. Churches have leaders but so do gangs. Martin Luther was a leader but so was Adolph Hitler.

Leadership skills aren't good or bad; it all depends on how they are used. Luther organized a religious movement and Hitler a holocaust—same skills.

Please understand that when I talk about being a leader, I mean being a Christian leader, a leader serving in ministry. If that's your calling, you'll find there are things required of you that aren't required if you're leading a company, a revolution, or a rock band.

I'd like to suggest that there are seven things you need to be if you want to possess authentic leadership in ministry. (I'll get to the list of things you need to do in the next chapter.)

1. YOU'VE GOT TO BE WILLING TO CHANGE.

Let me ask the same question I asked in the introduction. How badly do you want to be a leader? Are you willing to pay the price? The price tag includes changing how you think (since your actions come from your thinking); and it includes being willing to try new things. I am more open to trying different ways of doing things than at any other time in my life. I am only married to my wife; everything else is open and subject to change. I know people in ministry who are more comfortable with old problems than with new solutions. Are you willing to change how you think about yourself and your ministry? Are you willing to honestly admit your strengths and weaknesses? Are you willing to make tough choices based on what the Word of God says? You can't keep doing the same actions yet expecting different results.

I'm willing to make changes so that I can see results I've never seen in past seasons.

The question, friend, is are you willing to grow? If so, you have to learn to say yes to change.

2. YOU'VE GOT TO POSSESS INTEGRITY.

Integrity is uprightness of character that lines up with God's Word. It's being the same inside as you are outside—transparent through and through. To lead in ministry, you don't have to be right all of the time, which is a relief to me because I flunked the perfection test a long time ago! But you do need to give up the desire to have people *think* you're always right.

Admit it. We all like having people think we're right. It's just human, especially for leaders. We think it builds confidence in the troops when they see us make decisions and stand firm. But Old Jim cares more about what Father thinks of me than what people think of me. People respect a leader that they can see Jesus in more than a leader that is always large and in charge. The truth is we aren't always right. We're wrong . . . a lot. And nobody admires leaders who are too proud or scared to admit they don't know it all. Remember, it's not about you being right; it's about God being right and you leading in a way that points others to Him.

3. YOU'VE GOT TO BE FAITHFUL IN SMALL THINGS.

Faithful people handle small things well. They work with the resources they have, and they are careful stewards of those resources. If I've heard it once, I've heard it a hundred times: "If I had more budget, I'd be more effective."

My answer is this. No, you wouldn't. If you're not being faithful to serve others with the budget you've got, you don't deserve more. How you handle little things is exactly how you'll handle big things.

That principle holds for us leaders too. If you want to grow in your sphere of influence and responsibility, first do excellent work in handling the task at hand, and then you'll be rewarded with more.

When people join our servant-leader team at The Belonging Co, they don't start at the top. First, we want to see if they're faithful handling the small stuff. What if they were on staff at a bigger church? They still would have to start from a place of humility and servanthood—that's the heart of this house. Jesus lays out the principle in Luke

16:10, "Whoever can be trusted with very little can also be trusted with much, and whoever is dishonest with very little will also be dishonest with much."

We want faithful people on our teams because faithful people are committed to live out God's Word before they are placed in leadership. Faithfulness to steward what's entrusted will always brings success. Faithful people are committed to others, consistently serving the people God has placed around them. I have found that the best way to lead is from a posture of love and wanting God's best for others.

Faithful people get where God wants them, and they stay there, no matter what. They plug in and stay plugged in. They're dependable. They are planted deep!

Would the people who know you best say you're faithful? Why or why not?

4. YOU MUST BE A PERSON OF VISION, AND YOU MUST COMMUNICATE THAT VISION.

Proverbs 29:18 says, "Where there is no [vision], people cast off restraint; but blessed is the one who heeds wisdom's instruction." This highlights pretty clearly what happens when there's no vision in a person's life.

Having a great vision for your ministry is wonderful but not as wonderful as when a great vision has a hold of *you*. If, after prayer, you know in your bones that God wants your ministry to include kids from a neighborhood no other church is serving, the challenge of minding the details won't slow you down. You'll overcome any obstacle because you know for certain what God wants you to do. A great ministry vision is clear, focused, and captures your energy and imagination.

How to Give People Information in a Way That They'll Hear It

- Demonstrate your thankfulness and appreciation for each person you lead. Make this a policy—it's that important. Establish an environment of two-way communication and trust.

- Whenever possible, put all information in writing. Use email, text, website, video and whatever else is effective. Even when communicating orally at a meeting, also put key information in writing for distribution.

- Always explain *why*, as well as, *what*, and *how*.

- Ask those you lead if they understand what you're saying. Give others a chance to ask questions.

And when a great vision has a hold of you, sharing your vision will draw others to be a part of it because vision is contagious. People will line up to be on your team when they see they are part of a God-inspired vision, not just a job or task to complete. They'll stick because they care about what Father cares about.

What stops us in our ministry usually isn't a lack of people; it's a lack of people who understand and have bought in to the vision. No wonder people don't respond when we ask for their help—we haven't cast our vision in a compelling fashion so they can run with it.

Here's how that played out in my life. At my first church, I had a children's ministry of a whopping seven kids—six well-behaved kids and Little Bubba.

I'd come home from church and tell my wife, Julie, everything that had gone wrong that morning. Little Bubba did this, and Little Bubba did that. Little Bubba had grabbed Sally and smacked her up against the wall. Little Bubba had gone after Billy. I'd had to pick up after Little Bubba until I was about half crazy. But then when I'd ask Julie for her help in children's church, Julie would remind me once again that she wasn't remotely interested in helping me, thank you very much.

So I complained to the Lord about it, "Lord, this woman You gave me won't help me in my ministry. What's up with that? Can't You soften her heart or something?"

Well, the Lord asked me to listen to what I was saying to her, to listen to the words coming out of my mouth when I talked about what was going on in ministry.

I hadn't mentioned Kevin worshiping the Lord with all his heart or how Mary loved Jesus and prayed for her friends. I hadn't told Julie about the great things God was doing. I was too busy describing how little Bubba was terrorizing the class. I even made Little Bubba jokes:

Q: What's the best way to tell how bad Little Bubba's behavior will be this week?

A: See if there's a full moon.

I thought that stuff was *funny*. So my wife, based on what I said to her, thought of my children's ministry as a room full of Little Bubbas ready to take her hostage.

I knew what our ministry to children could become. I knew where Father God could take it for His glory. But I certainly wasn't communicating that vision to my wife. When I stopped to listen to what I'd been telling Julie, I realized I wouldn't have wanted to work with me either.

So I changed how I talked. I shared the good things that Jesus was doing in the lives of the kids, and within a few weeks, Julie asked me the big question.

"Does Little Bubba still go to our church?"

I said, "Yes, but last Sunday during praise and worship, he raised one hand halfway up. I believe revival has hit Little Bubba."

It wasn't long until one day she said, "You know, I think I'd like to help out."

In one moment, I doubled my workforce, and Julie and I got on the same team. That was a great moment. But it never would have happened if I hadn't started speaking the vision.

How do you describe to the people around you what your ministry looks like? What do your words and *attitude communicate*? Are you willing to lay aside complaining and cynicism and be relentlessly positive? Are you speaking the faithfulness of Father or the failures of doing ministry in your own strength?

5. YOU'VE GOT TO BE WILLING TO FOLLOW OTHERS.

Good leaders are also good followers. They submit to the authority God has placed in their lives.

I believe every person in ministry should lead in a way that reflects the heart, mission, and vision of those that they are under authority. If the pastor's vision for the church is to enter into a time of deepening discipleship, the other ministries should reflect and reinforce that purpose. If evangelism is the new focus, all should embrace that.

When we follow the leaders God has placed in our lives, we benefit from their wisdom and anointing. Think about a solider who's huddled in a foxhole while his squad is under enemy fire. He knows someone out there is shooting his direction, and he knows that if he keeps his head down, he's safe for the moment.

But then he hears his lieutenant shout, "Everybody up! We're moving forward!"

Those are not words a solider under fire likes to hear. But what the solider doesn't know is that his lieutenant was on the radio with headquarters. And headquarters knows from surveillance and reconnaissance that the enemy line is weakest straight ahead. *That's* the direction to go if the solider wants to survive.

By following his leader and charging forward, the solider benefits from information he couldn't get from the bottom of a foxhole.

Your pastor may well have more information than you have about where the Lord is taking your church. So if you're leading your area of ministry without being under your pastor's authority and leadership, you're in trouble.

In what ways are you following as you lead?

6. YOU'VE GOT TO BE UNPOPULAR AT TIMES.

Paul knew his young friend Timothy was going to be dealing with church people, so he wrote this to Timothy, "You then, my son, be strong in the grace that is in Christ Jesus" (2 Timothy 2:1).

Paul didn't advise Timothy to express leadership by pushing people around, demanding his own way, or manipulating people. The strength Timothy needed was to be strong in grace as he dealt with others and himself.

Leaders need that kind of strength because it's true—it *is* lonely at the top.

As a leader, you'll sometimes have to stand alone drawing lines not everyone is willing to cross. *Leaders aren't always popular.*

Back in the day, I grew up watching the *Miss America* pageant on television with my family, and I noticed the young lady who won the Miss America tiara seldom won the Miss Congeniality award. Apparently, doing what it takes to win the tiara doesn't necessarily make a candidate popular. That's true for leadership too. Few effective, strong leaders will end up in the running for Miss Congeniality.

Now, I care about people, and I want them to like me, but here's the truth. It really doesn't matter if they do.

Read through the gospels, and you'll see that Jesus didn't worry all that much about popularity either. Calling the local religious leaders a "brood of vipers" wasn't a move calculated to win friends.

Jesus called things the way He saw them. As a leader, you have to do the same thing, and that can be a quick ticket to Loneliness Junction.

Are you willing to make the unpopular calls—to stand alone when following God's leading requires it?

7. YOU'VE GOT TO BE SOMEONE PEOPLE SEE AS A LEADER.

If you want others to think of you as a leader, look like one. Carry yourself like one. Respond and react like one. Use your time the way leaders use their time— effectively. Handle criticism the way leaders handle it—by learning from it.

Put the principles and recommendations you find in this book into practice, and do it in full view of the people you lead. Your words, your love, your kindness, your willingness to always set the example for what you expect others to do communicate loud and clear that you're leading.

People haven't got any choice but to love you. The Bible tells them they're required to do that. But you've got to earn their respect.

Are you willing to do what it takes to help others see you as a leader? What's holding you back?

CHAPTER 3:
TEN LEADERSHIP FUNDAMENTALS

Authentic leadership is more than the potential to lead. It's even more than proven character in someone called by God to a leadership position. Authentic leadership is expressed in action too. It's one thing to talk leadership and quite another to demonstrate it.

Here are ten fundamentals you'll need to master—fundamentals we'll walk through together in more detail later in this book.

For now, let's do a quick overview to see how you're doing.

1. LEADERS SET AN EXAMPLE IN THEIR PERSONAL LIVES.

If you want people to follow you, give them something worth following.

As a leader, how you live your life—how you treat your spouse, how you treat your children, how you honor God—is far more important than where your name appears on an organizational chart.

One of the nicest compliments I ever received happened when my girls were teenagers. A dad at church number four walked up to me after church one Sunday. He said, "I've been watching how you get along with your teenagers. I want to take lessons from you. That's the relationship I want with my four-year-old when he gets to be a teenager."

I about started crying. Here was a man who believed that my relationship with my family was worth following. He saw us as an example.

How you follow your pastor sets an example too. I would love for everyone who serves in my ministry to treat me the way I treat my pastors. I set the example.

When my pastor calls a meeting, I'm not late. When my pastor wants to see me, I drop everything and get there. I don't check emails, texts, and missed calls when I'm talking with my pastor. My pastor is an authority in my life, and I communicate my respect by my actions. If you are attending a meeting on Zoom, pay attention; don't sit there and do other work. Be all in.

When it comes to leadership, the Golden Rule applies big time. You need to treat people in the way you want to be treated. How you treat your leaders and how you treat those you lead—it all matters. You're an example. Live as an example.

2. LEADERS ARE PROBLEM SOLVERS.

Leaders aren't derailed by problems. They meet challenges with a spirit of faith in God's ability to overcome those challenges.

I know it's popular to say that there are no such things as problems, just opportunities. Well, I'm here to tell you that now and then, Pastor Jim has problems.

When there aren't enough drivers for a field trip, that's a problem. When there's not enough budget to cover the growth you're experiencing, that's a problem. When a pipe breaks and floods the main auditorium, that's a problem.

And if you're the leader, people will expect you to solve those problems.

Leaders aren't afraid to get their hands dirty. They see that problems get solved. Period. They identify the problems and get them fixed. We'll take a look at strategies for whipping problems into shape in Chapter 10.

3. LEADERS SHOW INITIATIVE.

Leaders don't wait to be told what to do, nor do they shrink from challenges. They don't hide in their offices hoping things will get better when the bottom drops out of a program or when a chance to improve presents itself. They're proactive.

I'm a big believer in the "Santa" approach to making things happen around our church. As I walk around on Sundays, I make a list, and then I check it twice.

I may jot down that a particular greeter did a great job helping a new family feel welcome or that a teacher needs more training on how to present a Bible lesson to preschoolers. During the following week, I'll write a note to the greeter and see that the teacher gets some coaching.

Then the next Sunday, I will check to see that the greeter is still greeting and the teacher has improved. And as I go, I'm working on another list. I've always got a list of things to affirm, as well as, things to improve.

I've discovered that what I *expect* may or may not happen. But what I *inspect* gets done. So I inspect often. Do the same. Show initiative in fixing problems, shoring up weak spots, and celebrating strong performance.

4. LEADERS MANAGE THEIR TIME WELL.

We'll talk more about time management in Chapter 6 because if you can't manage your time, you'll be stuck reacting to people and situations. You'll never be effective. You'll never be an authentic leader. But with time management, you'll amaze even yourself.

Let me say right here that managing your time isn't just about getting lots of stuff done. It's about getting the *right* things done—the best things. And that means doing what *God* wants you to do.

5. LEADERS PATIENTLY DEMONSTRATE HOW THEY WANT THINGS DONE.

Authentic leaders strike a balance between showing and telling.

If all you ever do is tell people how to do ministry, they'll soon grow frustrated. They need to see it in action to really understand. But if you do all the work yourself and never explain what you're doing, they'll also fail to learn. You've got to both show and tell. Demonstrate and explain.

You'll know you've found the right balance when your workers can describe what you want because you've told them and they've seen you do it.

6. LEADERS INVEST IN OTHERS THROUGH COACHING.

Leaders come alongside people and help them get better at what they do. They become coaches.

A good coach starts with what a player can already do and builds on it. No football coach spends time teaching a quarterback how to tackle—that's not the quarterback's job. Of course, there are fundamentals everyone needs to know—the rules, how to catch, how to throw, but that's about it.

A wise football coach doesn't want each player to be equally good at every position. A wise football coach wants to make each player outstanding at whatever position that player fills.

What do your individual volunteers do well? Do you know? What's your individualized development plan for each volunteer in your ministry?

Sharpen your Apple Pencil. You've got some work to do. Write a development plan for each of the people who report directly to you in your ministry. Is it easy? No, but good coaching never is.

7. LEADERS TAKE APPROPRIATE RISKS.

Now and then it pays to be ignorant. I'm living proof.

During my first few years in ministry, back in the seventies, my church didn't have the money to send me to conferences. I'm glad because if I'd gone, I would have been told what I wanted to do was impossible.

You see, we had seven kids in our ministry. We wanted more kids. And we wanted kids to understand how they fit into our church.

I asked the Lord what we should do, and it seemed clear we were supposed to involve our kids in helps ministries. So back in the children's church, we plugged kids in as deacons, and we got kids involved in service as greeters, ushers, and worship leaders. Pretty soon we had more than three hundred kids, and soon after, I was invited to speak at those conferences I hadn't attended.

So I showed up, made my little presentation, and was confronted with lots of confused faces. It turns out that what we'd done wasn't supposed to work. It couldn't work, and people lined up to let me know it. Kids couldn't possibly do ministry. They'd never follow through; the whole model was sure to fail.

But when I got home, there it was . . . working!

I'm so glad I listened to the Lord instead of "thus saith the seminar speaker." Had we taken a big risk because we tried something new? Well, since we were following God's direction; no, not at all.

But even if we had moved ahead without a clear word from God, the only risk we'd taken was that of involving children in ministry. Sure, we'd risked a little bit of money, a lot of time, and my reputation. But most importantly, what if it had failed? We easily could have done something else to reach and disciple those kids.

What risks are you taking in your ministry?

8. LEADERS BEAR FRUIT AND GROW SPIRITUALLY.

Leaders carry more responsibility than followers and face greater challenges. They handle extra stress, extra work, and often make do with fewer resources than they wish they had. Those aren't ideal conditions for growth.

Yet even in difficult situations, leaders grow. They don't focus on what they're lacking; they focus on who they follow. And their faithfulness bears fruit in their lives.

How do you see yourself growing in your relationship with Father God? Are you deepening your commitment? Are you growing in love?

9. LEADERS DON'T WORRY ABOUT COMPARISONS.

People aren't in the church long before they realize that leaders come and go. And it seems they're always following a leader that they like better than you.

Don't worry about comparisons. You can't talk them into liking you better by pointing out the shortcomings of the person who was on staff before you. You have to do something that helps folks see you for who *you* are. But even that's not enough sometimes.

There are plenty of times I've come along behind someone else and looked pretty pale by comparison. But let me tell you about one of those rare times I was actually the guy who was used as a yardstick of excellence.

While I was on staff at church number one, my team and I had been particularly successful in launching some programs. I moved on from there, but once when I was back in town, I stopped by the church to see how things were going.

The children's pastor was gracious and invited me into his office. He shook his head and said, "If I hear one more Pastor Jim story, I'm going to throw up." He'd had way too many people tell him how it used to be and how I had done this or that.

I told the children's pastor the solution was simple—do something that works for him that I wouldn't have done. Something that Pastor Jim *couldn't* do. There were plenty of ministry programs I'd never been able to get up and running.

That's when the woman who ran the church's daycare center burst into the office. She said there was a crazy guy with a rifle out in the parking lot, and he was heading toward the preschool center's playground!

The children's pastor did the right thing. He picked up the phone and called the police. I did the stupid thing. I ran outside to see what I could do. I got to the parking lot, and sure enough, the daycare workers were quickly herding kids inside where they'd normally be safer, but the man with the rifle was already there.

I positioned myself between the kids and the man who was obviously disturbed. I said as sternly as I could, "Gimme that gun!"

He tossed it to me.

So I pointed and shouted, "Now get out of here!" He ran off. (You never know what you'll do in a situation like this until you get in it.)

No sooner was he out of sight when the police arrived. They were looking for a crazed-looking man holding a gun, and sure enough, there I was. I fit the description *exactly*.

Once we straightened out why they shouldn't shoot me (thankfully one of the officers attended that church and recognized me), the police sped off to look for the real trespasser while my knees shook at the thought of what I'd done. It turned out the man had escaped from a mental hospital, broken into a house, taken a gun, and was headed toward the playground for no apparent reason.

The children's pastor couldn't believe it. Just when he was about to come out from under my shadow, I'd shown up, faced down a gunman, and maybe saved a bunch of preschoolers. His life wasn't going to get easier anytime soon.

I don't share this story to show how big or strong I am. I was an idiot, pure and simple. It's God's grace that it worked out all right. I share this story because even with all that working against him, in time, that children's pastor established his own effective programs and put the "Pastor Jim stories" behind him.

So if someone can get past that, you can establish your leadership where you are. Give it some time, take action, and let God work through you.

With whom are you comparing yourself? What's the result? What if you could just put the comparisons aside?

10. LEADERS ARE LIFELONG LEARNERS.

Lots of professions require continuing-education classes. If you're a doctor or a nurse and you quit learning, sooner or later your license to practice medicine will be taken away from you. I wish we had something like that in local church ministry.

My background is children's ministry, and if you ask me, the kidmin world has way too many know-it-alls (people who hit on a successful idea and never grow past it). But the fact is they don't know it all. I know I don't, and the people I lead in individual areas of oversight are certain I don't. We've all got things to learn, and if you're not leading the way in learning, you can't expect the people you direct to keep learning and growing either.

I don't mean you need to get another degree. The place to start is to find a mentor— someone who's wiser and more experienced than you—and learn from them. Find someone you can go to ask questions. Then, listen to the answers and the questions that come back to you.

Working with a mentor is worth its weight in gold. You'll not only learn something, but you'll become teachable. And that's right where you need to stay.

Read books. Listen to podcasts. Join a coaching or masterclass group. Attend conferences. And be sure you tell your volunteers what you're learning. Your example says it's okay to admit you don't know it all. And it's okay to go find out what you need to know.

My mother taught me this—experience is the best teacher, but it doesn't have to be only *your* experiences that you learn from.

I visit other churches and learn from them. There's not a big church in this country where I haven't nosed around their website and their location to discover what they're doing and why.

If a church near you spent three months preparing a program that looked great on paper but failed miserably, wouldn't you want to know about that? I would. I want to learn from the experiences of others. That's a continuing education credit where someone else paid the tuition.

Leaders are lifelong learners. What have you learned lately?

CHAPTER 4:
THINK LIKE A LEADER

Authentic leadership begins with what you are and is then expressed in what you do. And somewhere along the way it changes how you think too.

You quit thinking like a follower. You begin thinking like a leader.

Thinking like a leader isn't just about having more information than the next person. Having information doesn't make you a leader. It makes you an encyclopedia.

Moses was a man who had plenty of information. He was raised by the Egyptians who were at the top of their game when Moses came along.

And Moses was raised not only by the Egyptians; he was raised by Egyptian royalty.

Moses was exposed to the best of everything—science, art, and culture. The Egyptians got the religion part wrong, but when it came to leadership training and problem solving, they had it nailed. Those pyramids didn't build themselves.

At the palace, Moses was trained to run the country. He was trained daily for leadership on a national scale. And sadly, that's not something Moses would have learned if God had left him in the Israelite culture.

The Israelites had a slave mentality—a follower mentality. For hundreds of years they'd practiced waiting for something to happen that would rescue them from slavery. While they get high marks for faithfulness, they weren't especially effective leaders. They weren't making anything happen.

So God plucked Moses out of Israelite culture and slave mentality and had him raised by Egyptians. God made a way for Moses' real mother to be there to teach him about the things of God. So Moses got the best of both worlds—an Egyptian education and religious training at the knee of his mother.

And even all that didn't adequately prepare and season Moses for the amazing leadership role God later gave him.

When God called Moses to ministry, Moses still had some things to learn about leadership. He still made mistakes. And if you're called into ministry, you'll have some things to learn about leadership as you go too. To start with, how do you think about leadership and your place as a leader?

In Exodus 3:11, we get an idea of how Moses viewed himself as a leader. God had just given him a very clear assignment: Go and bring My people out of Egypt. Moses replied, "Who am I that I should go to Pharaoh and bring the Israelites out of Egypt?"

Moses wasn't thinking like a leader. He wasn't even thinking like a follower. He offered excuses and questioned God's choice of messenger. Moses didn't want anything to do with the entire enterprise.

What had happened to the confidence Moses had as an adopted grandson of Pharaoh? It was gone. What had happened to Moses' willingness to obey God and do as he was told? It was nowhere in sight. Even when God supplied him with a plan, a helper, and a couple miracles to pull out as proof that Moses represented God, Moses shied away from the assignment.

Moses wasn't thinking like a leader . . . *yet.*

And maybe you're not thinking like a leader either.

Now, if you're reading this book, you're probably in a leadership position. God's entrusted some tasks or some people to your care. And you may be doing tremendous work, but are you thinking like a leader?

LEADERSHIP CHANGES HOW YOU THINK ABOUT YOURSELF

Maybe you grew up timid or you grew up like me—jumping into things headfirst without thinking. That's not leadership, by the way; it's recklessness. I'm lucky I lived through my childhood. God bless my mother; I think raising me ought to have gotten her a special medal. (God rest her soul.)

Leaders accept that they may have something to say when people are wandering around looking for direction. They share their ideas. They get involved in solving problems. They take responsibility. They know who they are based on what God's Word says. An authentic leader gets their identity from the truth of God's Word.

LEADERSHIP CHANGES HOW YOU THINK ABOUT OTHERS

When you think like a leader, you see that in many situations people want leadership to be expressed. It's not an intrusion. It's not arrogance. It's helpful.

Jesus called us all sheep in need of a shepherd. Hang around a church for a while, and you'll realize that people need considerable shepherding. Jesus is the Good Shepherd who can bring salvation, but we can be pretty good shepherds who bring order and structure—that's worth something too. An authentic leader thinks about others according to what God's Word says about others.

LEADERSHIP CHANGES HOW YOU THINK ABOUT YOUR OWN LEADERS

It's easy to question decisions made by your pastor or other leaders when you've got the benefit of hindsight. Making great decisions is easy when you have the luxury of thinking about the situation as long as you want.

But when you start thinking like a leader, you begin appreciating people who lead you. Authentic leaders quickly become better followers.

How we think about ourselves and our situations has a huge impact on our ability to lead. For God to use Moses as a leader, God had to help Moses overcome his slave mentality. In the church today, there are four other kinds of faulty thinking I've seen sabotage a leader's effectiveness in ministry. Do any of those sound familiar?

1. Faulty Thought: *"We've always done it this way."*

Okay, maybe you've never actually said those words aloud, but do you act like you believe them?

Why do you arrange your kids classrooms by age or gender? Why do you meet only on Sunday mornings? Why do you stick with the programs that quit being effective years ago? Is it because you've always done it that way?

I'm not suggesting we question the content of what we believe and teach. But when it comes to how we deliver that content, let's not let tradition stand in our way. Traditions can cost way more than they're worth.

I once served at a church that owned an organ donated by the family of a man who had died years before. The organ hadn't worked in years, and it sat right down front in the chapel where we did children's and youth ministry. And I mean right down front—it squatted on prime real estate and was always in the way.

As a musician, nonworking keyboards don't do much for me. I asked about fixing it and found out that parts were either unavailable or too expensive. There was no way we were ever going to get that organ working.

I asked if I could move the organ, and I was told there was no possible way. It had been donated by a church member. It was a memorial. It had been there for years.

I asked if I could take picture of the organ and put it next to a picture of the dead guy on a plaque. I could nail the plaque on a wall where nobody would trip over it. Wouldn't that work as a memorial too?

The board chewed on the idea awhile and decided that maybe, if I asked the surviving family members nicely and got their permission, something could be worked out. Perhaps.

I never got that organ moved. Years later the organ was moved, and the janitors recorded a video that I thoroughly enjoyed watching of it going away.

What traditions are hampering effective ministry in the ministries you oversee? They might not be as obvious as an old organ, so you'll need to give the question some thought. And it's possible that maybe you're the one perpetuating traditions that are slowing down your ministry. I've been guilty of that too.

2. Faulty Thought: *"Well, it worked for me."*

Why do we assume the way we learned about God is the best way for everyone to learn?

There's a little church out west where a woman has taught the two- and three-year-olds' Sunday school class for more than forty years. She even had the *pastor* in her class when he was that age.

Each week she gathers the children around a table, pulls out her flannel graph, and marches cutout Bible characters across the board as she tells stories. That's how she was taught, and she's not interested in doing Christian education any other way.

The children aren't allowed to touch the characters—kids literally have to *sit* on *their hands* during the Bible story so nobody's tempted to grab a sheep or apostle and play with it.

This woman's heart is in the right place, but her thinking is faulty. She's assuming everyone is wired just like her—that everyone learns the same way she learned. Because of that, she spends half her teaching time telling kids to sit still and stay quiet.

Authentic leaders are open to trying new approaches and new technology. They champion change if it helps accomplish the mission.

Are you able to lead others when it requires you to change? To try things that aren't comfortable? Please remember what I said earlier, "I am only married to my wife; everything else is subject to change."

3. Faulty Thought: *"Don't interrupt me; I'm busy leading."*

I've got a policy I try to live by: Pastor Jim doesn't like surprises. I mean, I *seriously* don't like them. If you're on my staff and something happens in your area of ministry, I should know about. It's your job to tell me—fast.

I don't want to be walking down the hall and get blindsided by an angry parent, angry teacher, or angry anyone else. And I don't want a problem to fester because nobody brought it to my attention.

I'll take the bad news along with the good. I can't think of one time that bad news went away because I ignored it. For leaders, ignorance is not bliss.

If you're going to lead, you've got to stay open and approachable. Do those words describe you?

Here's a test: Ask ministry peers how well you listen. How easy is it to give you bad news? What do they say?

It's especially important you make it very, very easy for people to give you bad news.

Otherwise you'll hear only the good stuff, and that's usually only part of the story.

How to Get People to Tell You Bad News

- **Don't shoot the messenger.** If you explode at the person who calls you Saturday night to report the sound system won't work, that's the last time anyone gives you a heads-up warning. You need to *thank* people who bring you bad news. Not the people who caused the bad news, but those who reported it. They're your early alert system.

- **Calmly ask questions, and dig deeper.** Here's what your messenger didn't tell you: The sound system doesn't work because half of it is missing. The youth group took it on their weekend retreat.

- **When you hear bad news, assume it's not the entire story.** There may be more bad news, and it's probably worse. Get the *whole* story before you respond.

- **Ask people who bring bad news to your attention what they recommend you do.** They've thought about the situation longer than you have, so get their opinion. You don't have to take their advice, but if you've got sharp people on your team, they may have already figured out a solution. The best way to raise up problem solvers is to ask them for solutions.

Some of the best ideas I've ever had are ideas I never had—the solution came from the wonderful people God has given me to lead and disciple.

4. Faulty Thought: *"I'm assuming this is true because nobody told me otherwise."*

When you're a leader and you're trusting information that's not true, you're deep in the weeds. Check and double-check your assumptions as you move into and through projects.

Maybe the pastor did say it was fine to have a pet in the children's ministry area so long as you cared for it. But if your pastor imagined a cuddly little hamster and you hauled in a rattlesnake; you are going to have conflict.

A mindset in which you assume everyone understands what you mean (or you assume everyone else shares your vision) is a disaster waiting to happen. Don't expect others to read your mind.

Check and double-check. Ask and confirm. You'll sleep better at night and so will everyone else.

Those four faulty thought patterns can destroy a leader's effectiveness. Avoid them. They're weeds in your garden—pull and toss them away.

SIX LEADERSHIP ATTITUDES

In place of those faulty thoughts, plant the following six attitudes I've observed in outstanding authentic leaders. Cultivate them, and you'll see your leadership flower and bloom.

Leadership Attitude 1: Think of yourself as a leader.

Look in the mirror: Do you see a leader looking back?

Look over your shoulder: Anybody back there counting on you to lead the way?

If God has called you to lead—even if you feel inadequate or uncertain—then lead. Use the influence God has given you to help others draw closer to Him and to do effective ministry. Decide to be faithful in the role God has given you. See yourself as God sees you. You are the leader Father has chosen and anointed for this task.

Leadership Attitude 2: Think of yourself as a servant and serve.

Effective leaders don't walk away from problems and challenges. They face them squarely. They don't float through life or walk past broken situations. They get involved.

That's because leaders believe they have something to contribute. Maybe they don't have a quick or easy answer, but they know that they can usually help. They know that they are problem solvers.

And more than anything, they know they are here to serve.

In what ways are you involved in your family's life? In your church? In your neighborhood? Your community?

When you don't know what to do in any situation, just look for ways to serve. Ask yourself how you can make this opportunity better. Always look for an opportunity to humble yourself and serve.

Leadership Attitude 3: See yourself as a follower too.

It's your job to follow your pastor's lead. If you ask your pastor how well you follow, what would you hear? What you *want* to hear is that you're leading others where the pastor believes God is taking the church.

Some leaders view themselves as trailblazing pioneers, boldly going where no one has gone before. If that is the case, they're going in the wrong direction. When faithful leaders lead, God has already gone before them, so they travel under the authority and with the permission of their leadership.

Leaders are proactive followers too. Set the example you want others to set. A few months ago here at our church in Nashville, I got to help someone take out the trash— several trips. In fact, I helped someone fill up a completely empty eight-yard long dumpster. Why was this so important? He had recently joined our staff, and I had recently become his supervisor. I saw an opportunity to model the heart of our house, our pastors's hearts, and how I wanted him to lead others. I could have told him what to do, but instead I chose to show him by modeling being a servant.

Leadership Attitude 4: Think outside the box.

It's great to respect traditions, but don't confuse them with Scripture. Be open to new information and methods. Look for better ways to accomplish your purpose and mission.

I'm not a spring chicken. I'm a white-haired guy who has been serving the church over the last five decades; and I'll tell you this: When I started in ministry, I didn't approach it the way I approach it today.

Things have changed. There weren't any computers, copiers, or even central air. There weren't text or email (there was regular mail, but ponies carried it from town to town). Young people didn't think as they think now or hit milestones in their lives as early as they do now. The culture was different. Families were different. I was different.

If I had dug in my heels at any time along the way and quit growing, I'd have quit being an effective leader. You will too. I am honored to lead alongside young leaders in their twenties, thirties, and forties. I am learning so much from them as I dare to explore new ways to do effective ministry.

How flexible is your thinking? How open are you to new ideas and methodologies?

Leadership Attitude 5: Think of conflict as natural.

Often we're so worried we'll hurt someone's feelings or that someone will get angry, we avoid confronting a problem. Authentic leaders value people's feelings, but they value getting what God wants done even more.

They know that when they lead, conflict will come with the territory.

The Bible doesn't spell it out, but I'm sure Moses heard all about why some of God's people couldn't leave Egypt. Somebody was sick or too old or about to give birth. Someone had questions about the route. A couple folks had already planned a birthday party, and they didn't want to reschedule.

But when it was time to go, it was time to go. Period. Like it or not, God's people were loading up the donkeys and heading out.

Conflict isn't the worst thing that can happen in your ministry. Apathy is. Conflict is simply an opportunity to get everyone to load up and move out, heading to a better place. Don't get me wrong; we should treat everyone from the posture of grace; but when conflict happens, extend grace, stay peaceful, and lead well.

Leadership Attitude 6: Think in organized ways.

It's the details that will trip you up every time—the receipt you didn't take a photo of for Expensify, the person you forgot to ask, the curriculum order you forgot to go online to download.

Leaders know they won't remember it all, so they keep a running list going. They write things down and cross things off. And they check and double-check whether something got done.

That doesn't mean authentic leaders are all naturally organized. Mercy, no! Some of the best leaders I've met have to write things down or they'd never get anything done. These are people who'd panic if they lost their phone because that little handheld computer contains their brain.

We must all care enough about our ministry and the people we serve to get organized and stay that way. An authentic leader is willing to learn new skills.

Do you love your ministry and the people you serve enough to take your organizational and management skills to the next level? To this decade?

I hope so because as we move through this book, that's exactly what you'll have the opportunity to do.

CHAPTER 5:
YOUR ROLE AS LEADER

No matter how long you're in ministry leadership, you'll always have one person reporting to you who can be, at times, impossible to lead. This person will find you on your worst days, test your patience as nobody else, and give you an opportunity to walk in grace again and again and again.

This person will keep your prayer life up to date just so you can manage well, but you won't be able to fire him or her. And even if you change churches a dozen times, this person will tag along.

That's because this person is you.

It's true with me. You see, I know what I'm capable of accomplishing. So I know when I don't give 100 percent to a project. I know when I've rolled over and slept in when I could have gotten up and exercised to build my stamina for service. I know when I stepped up to teach others, and I know when I wasn't well-prepared (or maybe too prepared). I know when I needed to rely on Holy Spirit but didn't. Nobody else may have known, but I knew.

By far, the worker in my ministry who's toughest to manage is me.

But that's where authentic leaders excel—*they manage themselves*. And that gives them the authority to manage others.

If you want to be successful in managing yourself in leadership, a place to begin is defining your role as a leader. What's your job? What *isn't* your job? Does the job description your church handed you line up with the job description God has given you in Scripture? If not, get your written job description changed right now; it's going to get in your way, and it certainly will not help you.

First Peter 5:2 says, "Be shepherds of God's flock that is under your care, watching over them—not because you must, but because you are willing, as God wants you to be; not pursing dishonest gain, but eager to serve."

If you're a ministry leader in a local church, God has handed you two jobs—shepherd and overseer. You've got both those roles to fill, no matter what's on your job description.

THE ROLE OF OVERSEER

You're supposed to make sure that stuff gets done—that's what an overseer does. And you're supposed to make sure the flock God has entrusted to you gets fed, watered, and cared for. That's what a shepherd does.

But years ago, where I got into trouble, I thought in children's ministry, the flock I was supposed to oversee was just the children. What I soon realized was that kids weren't the majority of my flock. The kids in my ministry were being cared for by the leaders I had trained. *My* flock was also the adults who were shepherding the children. That's who I needed to work with most closely as I equipped them to do ministry.

Huh? Work with grown-ups? But you were in *children's* ministry! Why couldn't you just go work with kids and let someone else worry about preparing the annual budget, evaluating and training staff, writing the strategic program for outreach, and meeting with the pastor and other leaders on staff?

Because that's your job, Bub. You're the overseer.

Maybe you have always hated math and you're scared of pulling together a budget, so you've delegated the job of filling in the spreadsheet; but remember it's still your responsibility. You're responsible for creating programs that drive the budget.

Effective overseers don't duck core responsibilities or dodge making key decisions. They stay engaged, even if tasks are delegated. They provide oversight.

Look, if the notion of stepping back from working with people with boots on the ground so you can work with other leaders doesn't sit well with you, I feel your pain. I love to preach to a room full of people. I love to teach and spend time with our church family at large. But anymore, preaching and teaching are the easiest things I do in ministry.

What's hard is getting all the stuff done *before* I can preach and teach.

Somehow the room has to be prepared—carpets cleaned, floors swept, chairs lined up, music selected and rehearsed. Materials have to be chosen, ordered, paid for, and put in the hands of servant leaders who've been recruited and trained. Decisions have to be made that align each ministry I lead with the larger ministry of the house. Somebody has to make all that happen.

And I'll tell you this: It can't always be just me.

In fact, it shouldn't be just me. I'm an overseer. My job isn't to do everything but to make sure everything gets done with excellence. If I'm doing it all myself, I'm not doing my job; I'm crowding other people out of the jobs they're supposed to be doing.

If I could change one thing about young pastors and other ministry servant leaders, it would be this: I'd teach them that they *shouldn't do it alone.*

Time and time again I've visited churches where particular ministries are a one-person show. There's someone upfront who's doing it all herself. She greets folks at the door, leads the praise and worship time, and operates the sound and lights. She presents the lesson, sings the special music, then picks up the sheep droppings that didn't make it home when the service is over.

And what's wrong with that? At least she knows everything will be done—and done right. That's the benefit of doing it yourself.

The problem is that because she's doing it alone, she's created an environment where the fruit of her labor won't last. If she leaves, there goes the program with her—right out the door.

I get to visit with lots of church ministry leaders who attend conferences. It breaks my heart when I look out at a crowd and realize the same churches as last year are back, but eighty-five percent of the faces are different. The leadership has almost completely turned over because people tried to do it all themselves and burned out. They're gone. And they took the ministries they created with them when they left.

When you try to do it all yourself, you are signing up for burnout. Period. End of story. You simply can't avoid it.

Think about the ministries you lead. If you're a one-person show, get used to the idea that you won't last for the long haul.

And here's a question for you: *Why* are you in that spot? Is it because the Lord has surrounded you with talentless, passionless people who won't do ministry? You've tried and tried but nobody will come alongside you to help?

Or is it that you're not really inviting others to participate?

I know this: God hasn't put you in the pool to drown. There's someone somewhere who will carry part of the load you're shouldering. Is there a chance that you're not inviting that person—or those people—to step up and help?

You're to be an overseer. Your job is to find people and equip them for ministry. Your job is *not* to do everything yourself.

Are you willing to be an overseer? To fulfill that administrative leadership role? To recruit, train, and manage others who'll work with those you are ministering to?

Sadly, most ministry pastors I know aren't willing to be overseers.

Some of them don't think they have the background, education, or temperament to be in charge. "I don't mind helping out the pastor by running a part of the program," they'll say, "but I don't want to be the one who's responsible for the whole thing."

Guess what? You are responsible. The question is whether you'll grow into the skills to be effective in meeting that responsibility.

As a longtime children's pastor, I had to be willing to share leg-hugs from boys and girls with everybody else. But I learned that some of the teachers I've trained over the years are every bit as good a pastor as I am, even if they don't have the title. They like getting those hugs too. When instead of doing it myself, there are three or thirty or three hundred of us doing ministry every week, guess what? A whole lot more ministry gets done. My team doesn't always do ministry exactly the way I'd do it, but that's all right too.

If you're doing it all yourself, make sure it's not because your own perfectionism or ego is in the way of God calling others to get on board.

Remember, it's part of your calling to raise up and train others to do ministry. You can't do that if you're unwilling to give up some control.

If you're going to be an overseer, it's time to identify what you are doing that someone else can do, and start pouring your heart for ministry into others and let them do ministry with you.

SHEPHERDING THE FLOCK

I believe our first priority as a leader is to feed and care for the sheep God has entrusted to us. I mean, you may run a dozen great programs, but programs aren't going to last forever. Even the best programs will be gone in a few years.

But people? God made people for eternity.

I won't pretend to provide you with everything you need to be an effective people helper. I've got friends who are outstanding pastoral counselors, and they still get stumped frequently. It's a challenge to come alongside people and give them what they need to be contented, growing, faithful sheep. If you're overwhelmed at the thought of guiding your volunteers into a deeper relationship with God, you're probably right. You *should* feel overwhelmed—and let that send you straight to God for strength and guidance.

Be an overseer who equips others to do the shepherding.

Finally, when you're managing your role as leader, don't forget to take care of this . . .

MANAGING YOUR WORKLOAD

I've got some bad news for you: You have limitations. You can't do everything. Sooner or later you've got to rest.

I see you smiling. Maybe it's because you don't really believe that. You thrive on the energy of ministry or doing the impossible. You'd pull three all-nighters in a row if you could figure out how to sleep with your eyes open.

Fatigue is part of the cost of being in ministry, right?

No, it isn't. And when you try to stretch yourself too thin, you end up hurting other people in addition to hurting yourself.

I was on a three-hour flight with a guy whose company supplies T-shirts and wearable accessories for Disney. This guy ran his multi-million dollar business from an office high in the Empire State Building. When it came to financial security, he'd arrived.

I was telling him about going shopping with my daughters, and he laughed. "I never shop with my kids. My assistant does the shopping for me."

I probed a bit, and he finally explained that he couldn't take them shopping, even if he'd wanted to do it. "My kids hate my guts," he admitted. "Even my wife hates my guts."

How sad. He'd poured his life into building his company, but he'd lost his family in the process.

I wish I could tell you that never happens in ministry, but it does. All of the time. So many family tragedies could be avoided if people like you and me would manage our workload.

Don't count on your supervisor or pastor to set your limits for you. It'd be nice if they notice and helped you work reasonable hours, but they might not notice you're headed for burnout until it's too late. Don't expect the people you serve to tell you to slow down either. It's up to you.

It's your responsibility to manage yourself and your workload. The next few chapters will give you some ideas for how to do just that.

CHAPTER 6:
MANAGING YOUR TIME

Of all the resources you can spend to accomplish things, time is the most valuable. Why? Because it's the only one you can't get more of.

If you run over budget, you can always ask for a few extra bucks. But the hours you've spent are gone. So it makes sense for you to be intentional on how you manage time—yours and that of your staff and volunteers.

I'm not suggesting you get a stranglehold on your time so you can do nothing but work. I know people like that—they rush between meetings with a smart phone in one hand and a smoothie in the other.

The goal of time management isn't to set a new world record for how much you can get done. It's to figure out how to get the most important stuff done—and that includes time off.

Here's a truth: People who manage their time well can work fewer hours, not more. They aren't rushing to the church at midnight to take care of something they forgot to do. They know which projects are going well and which ones are in trouble *before* a crisis develops.

If you get your time under control, you can take off the days you have allotted to be off and still get things done.

FOUR KEYS TO MANAGING YOUR TIME

Here are four skills that will help you get more done than you thought humanly possible.

1. Planning

Get yourself a good calendar, and write down how you want to spend your time. Fill it in a year in advance (or longer if possible).

Start with the events you know happen every year—the programs, the big events, camp, etc. Write in everything you know already. Get them all down so you know at a glance when you're likely to be busy. For example, we do a staff retreat every January, an Egg Hunt the Saturday before Easter, a Servant Leader Conference in April, and a Servant Leader Christmas Party the first Friday in December.

Now add other things you need to remember such as holidays and school breaks. The families in our church come from multiple districts with different spring breaks and different school-year starts and ends. That's handy information when I'm figuring out when to have camp and start Summer Hangs!

Write down staff training and planning sessions too. If you meet regularly with your ministry leadership, get those down on the church shared calendar. Write down every recurring meeting you're expected to attend. For example, we do a team night for all our servant leaders each month on the last Thursday.

Finally, put in your anniversary, the birthdays of family members, and if you usually go on vacation the same time each year, get that down.

Your calendar is pretty full, isn't it? Well, it's about to get *more* full.

Now figure out the deadlines you'll need to hit to get your ministry ready for each event. If your Fall Kickoff is the first week of August, you'll need to order supplies in July. If you want to rent an inflatable game, you'd better call and reserve it in March. Fill in the steps you need to take to pull off each event.

I can hear you now: "Jim, I'm just not that organized. I can't keep all those steps straight."

Hey, I'm not naturally that kind of person either. That's why I use a calendar. Lord knows enough things come up that I can't possibly plan for, so I want to plan those that I can plan. Then the only thing I have to do is check my calendar every day, so I've got a hope of being organized. I don't want to find myself two weeks before the Fall Kickoff realizing it's too late to pull it together. Your mind is for dreaming and thinking, not for remembering—that's what your calendar is for.

Don't put your calendar away yet because you're about to add the really important stuff. You can't afford to miss appointments with . . .

The Lord—I'm not spiritual enough to get up at 5:30 a.m. every day to pray and read the Bible. It's not going to happen. But before I go to bed each night, I set an appointment for the next day to spend time with the Lord. Let's say 3:00 p.m. works for me to spend time with Jesus. If someone calls and asks, "Can I meet you at 3:00?" I say, "I already have an appointment then. How about 4:00?" Nobody gets offended.

Do not skip reserving time for prayer. Being faithful to know, love, and follow God is the most important thing you can do with your time!

Your Family—I'm a family man before I'm a pastor, so I put birthdays on my work calendar. My anniversary is there. So were piano recitals, dates with my wife and daughters and grands, and all other significant family events. I block off that time, and I defend it. A great evaluation question is, "Are you married to your family and dating the church, or are you married to the church and dating your family?"

My family members don't get offended if they see I've scheduled an appointment with them. That doesn't mean I'm unavailable other times; it means that in addition to wanting to be with them other times, I've made a point to be available at special times.

Daily Life—There are things in your life that will take time next month. You don't know what they all are just yet, but they'll show up—guaranteed.

If you've booked every hour solid, what will you do when a toothache gets your attention? When your car breaks down? When a sick child needs you? Smart time managers don't schedule each and every hour; they anticipate interruptions and crises, and they leave time to deal with them.

Do this: Block out a few hours each day, and write down the word *people*. Sometimes those people will be leaders who want coaching, your pastor who has a great idea to discuss, or a young person who needs a hug and an ice-cream cone after losing a volleyball game. Build in room for interruptions.

Also, building in time for the leaders you're helping to develop. I reserve lunches for meeting with people who report to me and those whom I'm discipling. I don't just meet people at restaurants. If at all possible, I arrange to go with them to the place we're eating. That gives us more time together. We can talk openly in the car without worrying if someone can overhear us. That can be a problem in a restaurant. We also have the ride back to go over action steps.

2. Preparation

This is where you quit writing down what you want to accomplish and get busy figuring out how to make sure you get it done. You've already set deadlines on your calendar, but how will you make sure you meet them?

Carrying a to-do list goes a long way in helping you manage your time. It can be as simple as an index card you tuck into your pocket or as cool as an app on your smart phone. (My favorite is Todoist, but I also like Asana.) Check it often during the day so you can stay on track.

When do you need to get that monthly expense report turned in? How will you collect numbers, mileage, and receipts? Put systems in place, or you'll never get it done. I use Expensify at church, home, and for Jim Wideman Ministries.

Good preparation is the step that separates calendar-keepers from *effective* time-managers.

This is the time to ask the question: Did you *really* fill in the step-by-step deadlines that will help you get next year's VBS done in a timely fashion? If you didn't, go back and do it now. If God has promised to direct your steps, why are you not thinking in steps?

When will you pick a theme? Order curriculum for review? Meet with your VBS leaders and your recruitment chairman? When will you train volunteers? Start the sign-ups?

Sort out the tasks in logical order, and get them on your calendar; otherwise, your planning calendar isn't worth much. Reminders really make a big difference.

3. Evaluation

This is when you stop writing down how you want to spend your time and start writing down how you actually spend it.

Trust me: this exercise will open your eyes. You don't even need a calendar; just keep a running log going on a sheet of paper.

How much time did you talk on the phone exactly? With whom and about what? How much time did you spend binging on Netflix, surfing the web, or checking your Facebook?

"But I'm on Facebook for work." Well, it's also a great place to waste time.

"But Jim, I *have* to watch the news."

No, you don't. I gave up watching the news when my daughters were little, so then I could play Barbie dolls with them. I asked myself: Is it more important to know who is bombing whom, or whether Whitney had a good day in school?

Now my daughters don't play Barbies anymore; those days have long gone. They're both boy moms now. And I still want to know how they're doing, how their husbands are, as well as, how those precious grand boys are doing.

The reason to evaluate how you spend your time is so you can spend it the way God wants you to spend it. Remember, you won't get even one minute back. You've got to be a good steward of your time.

When you check your week's log, identify the time wasters—tasks that didn't help you accomplish anything worthwhile. Were you focused or just filling hours?

If you'll save one hour per day, over the course of a year, you'll free up two full weeks of twenty-four-hour days. That's forty-two eight-hour work days. That's some powerful motivation!

Here's what I do: Every night before I go to bed, I look back at the day. I ask myself how I used my time and what I can change that will make me more efficient the next day.

Years ago I walked by a pay phone (if you don't know what this is, Google it) with a sign taped above it that read: "Business Phone: Please limit calls to three minutes."

Somehow that image has never left me, and then it dawned on me: The phone on my desk at church is a business phone. Even the cell phone in my pocket is a business phone. When I pick up the phone, I have a timer on my watch that's set for five minutes. I do my very best to end that call before the timer sounds.

It's not that I want to be mean or cold; it's that I want to be efficient. *Most calls can comfortably be ended in five minute or less*—the rest of the time is wasted. This habit has saved me hundreds of hours to be used elsewhere.

Every night I also ask myself how to be more effective the next day. What should I be focusing on? What needs to be accomplished first?

Again, the idea behind managing your time isn't to figure out ways to squeeze more activity into the day. The goal is to do the right things and to do them efficiently. That's good stewardship.

4. Delegation

Since we all have the same amount of hours in a day, the only way to get more time at our disposal is to use the time of others.

What are you doing that someone else could do? What are you doing that's keeping you from doing what *only* you can do?

It dawned on me one day that I'm not the only guy who can straighten chairs. I realized my Sundays were packed with things that others would gladly do—if I would train others then delegate the responsibility and authority to handle those tasks. It freed me to spend time with people, meet new families, and so many other things that I needed to do.

Here's what I've learned about using the time of others: *Request weekly reports.*

Which numbers does your pastor want to see each week? Attendance? Giving? Conversions? Ask volunteers to provide those numbers to you from their areas of ministry, and decide what else you want to know.

I have four questions I ask my paid staff every week:

1. Which families and leaders did you spend quality time with?

2. What did you do for leadership development?

3. Is there anything you know that I need to know?

4. Is there anything that I know that you need to know?

Four simple questions but the answers tell me what's happening, what information people need, and what my staff is doing to grow themselves, as well as, to grow others. And the answers to those four questions help me assist my staff in setting priorities for the coming week. I know what they're planning, so I can provide guidance to keep their priorities lined up with my priorities and with my pastors' priorities.

COMMUNICATE IN WRITING WHENEVER POSSIBLE.

Churches have way too many meetings. We even meet to come up with which meetings we need! Almost every volunteer I know can read, so I use emails and text as much as possible. I go out of my way to avoid meetings. That means:

1. We have time to get some real work done.

2. When I *do* call a meeting, people know it's important, so they show up.

I don't hold meetings that don't involve everyone because it's a waste of time to pull everyone together when I really want to talk just to the registration workers or the new teachers. I'm selective about whom I invite to meetings, and we cover specific materials aimed just at them.

Use these tips to keep meetings from consuming your calendar (and life):

- **Schedule as many meetings as possible during the day, not in the evening.** Ask people to meet you for breakfast. It costs a few dollars, but you'll keep your evening free for family.

- **If you must have an evening meeting, schedule it on a night that people are already coming to church.** It minimizes strain on your volunteers . . . and you.

- **There's no such thing as a perfect meeting time.** There's always someone who can't make it. Always have a plan for distributing information to no-shows. That's why I like Zoom meetings—no childcare needed, no drive time, and you can record them. These days I like to give an in-person, as well as, an online option.

- **Provide food.** Volunteers appreciate it when you say, "Just come early to church, and I'll feed you and your kids." They have to eat anyway, so meeting over a mealtime isn't as big of a deal.

- **Plan recurring meetings the same time each month.** It helps the planning-impaired people on your team.

- **Be efficient.** Advertise a starting time and an ending time. Start on time. End on time. Never run over. If you realize you can't cover everything on your agenda, cut items from your agenda.

- **Allow time for questions.** If a question doesn't pertain to the whole group or the subject discussed, address the questions privately following the meeting. Stay as long as you're needed. Realize that sometimes people won't ask a question or make a comment in front of others.

- **Make sure people know what they're to do.** Before you adjourn the meeting, repeat clearly the action steps and assignments that have been given during the meeting.

- **Don't waste people's time.** When conducting a meeting that includes people from different ares of responsibility, first go over the items in the agenda that pertain to the whole group. Then dismiss everyone who isn't involved with the other agenda items.

When you must have a meeting, distribute an agenda in advance.—Agendas help you stay on task at meetings. They eliminate rambling and keep everyone focused, and advance agendas help people prepare.

Do this for me: If someone invites you to a meeting, request an agenda up front. How else will you know whether or not you should attend?

Of course, if it's your pastor calling the meeting, just go. Your pastor is the agenda.

DON'T TREAT ALL VOLUNTEERS EQUALLY.

Here's a harsh fact that bothers some ministry leaders: It's smart to be with who you are spending time with.

Jesus didn't spend an equal amount of time with each disciple. Peter, James, and

John got way more than their "fair share" of Jesus' time, and maybe every now and then the other disciples got jealous.

But Jesus invested His time in people who moved His mission and purpose forward. He never apologized for having an inner circle. You don't need to apologize either.

Not every volunteer wants to spend more time with you. Some are already booked solid, and others aren't interested in deepening their skills and commitment. They're marginal volunteers.

But there are people who want training and discipleship. They want to grow. They want to stick with serving in the ministry they are passionate about. Those are the people who you can most profitably invest your time in.

Who are the people in your inner circle?

MAKE PEOPLE TAKE TIME OFF.

Sometimes I tell people who work with me, "Go home. You shouldn't be here at this hour." I literally throw them out of the building for a day or two.

Volunteers and staff can work themselves into a state of exhaustion thinking that they are helping you and the church and that they are honoring God. When they burn out and drop out of ministry, the leadership team shakes their heads and wonder why.

But I'll tell you why: They're tired!

Ministry is a marathon, not a sprint. You're in it for the long haul, not just until class ends. Even convicts get time off for good behavior. Shouldn't the people you direct?

MAKE THINGS EASIER FOR YOUR STAFF AND SERVANT LEADERS.

Offer help. Streamline and simplify procedures. Look for ways you can make serving in your ministry painless.

Now and then I ask my staff the following questions:

- What should we stop? (For example, a program that's become obsolete or is no longer effective.)

- What could we change that will make doing ministry quicker, easier, or cheaper?

Remember, it doesn't take leadership to stop something that's not working, but it does take leadership to change something that's working and make it work even better and more efficient.

Ask people who work in the trenches what would make their lives easier. When I'm considering how to change the nursery check-in policies, I don't make that decision myself. I call up the little lady who does it week after week, and I say, "If you were in charge, what sort of changes would you make?"

Then I do what she says. She knows. She's living it. She's got a better handle on the nursery than I have from sitting in my office.

FIND EQUIPMENT AND TECHNOLOGY THAT HELPS YOUR TEAM.

What technology could solve your volunteers' problems? Would faster printers and more iPads make the check-in desk hum along at three times the speed? Would ProPresenter, Planning Center, or an AppleTV in each classroom remove stress from the lives of those you lead?

Provide the tools your people need to be effective and efficient. You'll have happier people, and they'll have more time to be available.

MOVE PAST DELEGATION TO DUPLICATION.

It's good when you delegate because then you've got someone representing you and acting on your behalf.

But *duplication* is even better. Duplication is training your team members to do what you can do. They have your heart for ministry. You've coached them until they're a copy of an original—you.

There's no success without a successor. Who's your successor? Who can do what you do (and maybe do it better)? And who is *that* person training? If you don't know, it's probably not happening.

If there were two of you, you'd have way more time to meet your ministry goals. Well, there isn't any reason that there can't be two of you . . . or twenty.

TOP TEN LIST FOR MASTERING TIME MANAGEMENT

Here's a quick list of the skills you need to be a certified time manager.

10. Account for your time. Do you know how you spend your day? List it, and evaluate it.

9. Plan your time offensively. Remember, your time belongs to you. Make a to-do list. Don't automatically say yes when someone asks you for a meeting.

8. Keep your priorities in order. Administer triage with every situation that comes your way. Deal with the big stuff and the timely stuff first.

7. Delegate to faithful, capable people. What are you doing that someone else can do? Teach someone how to do it, and then check in to ensure success.

6. Plan for interruptions. Things won't go exactly as planned; leave room in your schedule to deal with surprises.

5. *Respond* rather than *react* to crises. There are always two (or more) sides to a story. Stay calm and get the facts—*then* make a decision.

4. Don't procrastinate. Don't put off the things you dread.

3. Get help. You don't have all the answers, so find some people who can help you get them. Make a call. Read a book. Seek out a mentor or coach.

2. Plan for growth. People follow a leader who has a plan. What's your plan for growing spiritually, organizationally, and numerically?

1. Pray. Things happen in you and in your ministry that won't happen any other way than when you pray.

Want to learn even more about time management? Check out my book *Beat The Clock*. Go to www.jimwideman.com, and order yours today.

CHAPTER 7:
YOUR ROLES, PRIORITIES, AND GOALS

It's easy to feel intimidated when you start thinking about roles, priorities, and goals. They sound so important and permanent.

Let me make it easy for you with a seven-step process:

1. IDENTIFY YOUR ROLES IN LIFE.

Maybe you're a parent, a son or daughter, a husband or wife, a Christian, and a leader. You may also be a student and a small-group leader. These are all roles. Write down all the roles you fill in life in any order that they come to mind.

This is a book for ministry leaders, but which ministry you are a leader of is probably just one role on a very long list of roles. You might wonder why I'm asking you to write down *all* your roles.

I've seen ministry leaders practically ignore their own families so they can help other families at church. They miss their own kids' piano recitals so they can attend other kids' events. A person can do a great job filling the ministry-leader role, while the role of parent suffers terribly.

So I think it helps to look at *all* your roles—everything you could be doing—so you can decide which roles are most important. You're just human. You can't do everything, so you have to make choices.

2. CIRCLE THE IMPORTANT ROLES.

I know: Your roles are all important. That's why you're doing them. But they're not all equally important.

Circle any role you listed that only you can do. For instance, if you have *volunteer firefighter* and *mother* listed, circle *mother*. That's because no matter how important it is to be a volunteer firefighter, someone else could do it. But nobody else can be your child's mother.

Now circle any role that is absolutely required to faithfully follow Jesus. It's your purpose in life to be faithful, so let's make sure *Christ follower* is circled. And if you're called to children's or youth or any particular ministry, circle that as well.

Just because *square dancer* isn't circled doesn't mean you can never do-si-do again. A balanced life includes doing some things just for fun or movement.

But when push comes to shove, the roles you've circled are the real important ones —your gotta-do list. Everything else is icing on the cake. That might mean you give up square dancing, at least for this season in life. (Some of you Generation Z folks may need to Google that one.)

For me, I had to step back from music. I love playing guitar. I went to the Rock and Roll Hall of Fame in Cleveland my first time and wanted to just move on in. On my list of roles in life, you'll find *GUITAR PLAYER* in big, block letters.

But I'm also a daddy. And a husband. And "G." And I do several other things that require time and energy. I just can't justify sitting in my man cave practicing three hours a day or playing in a band every weekend, even at church.

So for now, I work when I should, and I play when the opportunity arises. *GUITAR PLAYER* is still on my role list, but it's not circled.

3. PRAY ABOUT YOUR CIRCLED ROLES.

Get a fresh sheet of paper, and list your circled roles. These are the roles in life that will define you, and it's time to do some soul searching.

You need to know if your must-do roles, as you see them, match up with what Father God wants you to be doing. God's plan often differs from our own plans.

Proverbs 14:12 says, "There is a way that appears to be right, but in the end it leads to death." There are some serious consequences to missing God's plan for our lives.

Do your roles line up with the Word of God? If you've got a spouse, and your role of husband or wife isn't circled, you're in trouble, and not just with your spouse. You're in trouble with God, who joined you and your spouse together. He expects you to do everything possible to protect and further that marriage relationship. It's important.

Paul writes in 2 Corinthians 5:9 that the One we need to be pleasing most is God: "So we make it our goal to please Him, whether we are at home in the body or away from it."

Pray about your list. Do the roles you've chosen honor and please God?

4. DECIDE HOW YOU'LL LIVE OUT YOUR ROLES.

Now it's time to define your roles.

If you've written *mother*, jot down ideas for what it means to be a first-rate mom. Does it mean being involved in your child's education? Serving on the PTA? Home schooling? Ask Holy Spirit to guide you as you dream about filling that role with excellence.

Clarify every role you've circled. What does it mean to be an excellent children's or youth ministry worker? Are you a doer or a delegator? A coach or a leader? A trainer or a teacher in the classroom? Get it down on paper.

Talk about this with people who matter to you. Ask your kids how they define an excellent parent. What does your spouse think it means to be an excellent husband or wife? Ask your boss what it means to be an excellent employee. And ask your leader to define what it means to be an excellent ministry leader. Why? Because you're at the church to serve your leaders, so it's just smart to find out if your ideas line up with your leaders' ideas.

Spend time getting role definitions down on paper because those definitions are your marching orders.

Here's how it works: Suppose you circled *parent* as a top role, and then you decide that being actively involved in shaping the spiritual life of your children is one part of how you define that role. So how do you accomplish that?

You could start by making sure you get your kids to church, but that's not enough.

You might also decide to talk with your children daily about how they saw God working in their lives. You may decide a time of family prayer each day will help you shape their hearts for God. How about a weekly family night to make your family a priority?

Those four specific action steps will help you fill the role of parent with excellence. You'll probably come up with another thirty things you could do, but you can't do them all, all the time. So do this: Circle the five or six most important things you could do to fill your parent role with excellence. If on a busy day, you can only squeeze in five or six of your thirty or forty action steps, which five or six would you pick?

Those are your top priorities. They're the things you most want to do—and they'll help you fill roles God wants you to fill.

See how going through this process helps you have a purposeful, focused life? You can identify and do the most important things to fill your most important roles. You can make a difference in the lives you touch!

5. LOOK TO THE NEXT WEEK . . . MONTH . . . YEAR.

How will you stay on target and focus on your top priorities—those actions that help you fill important roles? Life's full of distractions, and it's easy to quit doing what's important because you're taking care of urgent things.

You stay on target by creating—and meeting—goals.

A goal is a statement describing what you want to accomplish. "I want to be an excellent parent" is a goal but not a very useful one. For a goal to actually help you accomplish one of your priorities, it has to include these elements:

- *Be specific.* "I want to be an excellent parent by *tucking my child into bed and praying with them*" is specific.

- *Make it measurable.* You can tell if you've tucked a child into bed. You've either done it or you haven't.

- *Keep it attainable.* You need to be able to actually do it. "Flap my arms, and fly to Toledo" is a goal, but I doubt you can do it.

- *Make it time oriented.* "I want to be an excellent parent by tucking my child into bed and praying with them *at least five times a week*" is realistic and time oriented. You can write the activity on a calendar to remind you to do it until it becomes a habit.

Do this: For each of your top priorities, set some goals. You want to be an excellent parent? Tucking your child into bed and praying with them five nights a week might be an appropriate goal. So might taking your child to church at least once per week. Set goals that support your priorities, and tweak them until they're specific, measurable, attainable, and time oriented.

Write the goals onto your calendar and to-do list so you actually complete the tasks. They're helping you live out your most important God-given roles. What else is more important to do each day?

6. FIND SOMEONE TO HOLD YOU ACCOUNTABLE.

It may be your pastor or supervisor, a mentor, coach, or your spouse. Friends are great accountability partners if they're willing to tell you the truth—and if you're honest with them.

Give this person—or these people—a copy of your top roles, your priorities (what has to happen to do the roles with excellence), and your goals (specific action steps to help you accomplish your priorities). Ask people who are holding you accountable to check in with you every month to find out where you need help and where you need prayer.

7. WRITE A DATE IN YOUR CALENDAR, OR SET A REMINDER TO REVISIT THIS PROCESS.

Things change, so decide now when you'll go back through this process. The second, third, and fourth time through won't take as long, and it's worth the effort. I suggest you revisit your roles and priorities once a year to see if any need revising.

You'll have to revisit your *goals* far more often. Sometimes the things you need to do to be an excellent ministry leader change quickly, and the changes aren't initiated by you.

When I went to work with Pastor Willie George at church number four, I quickly learned to listen for three words Pastor Willie would say on a regular basis: "I've been thinking."

When Pastor Willie said, "I've been thinking," it meant that we were fixing to get real busy, real soon. My goals were about to change.

Sometimes those three words meant a third or fourth service was coming. Sometimes it meant some big events were on the horizon, or more staff was about to be added. It's amazing how those three words got translated differently every time he said them. And no matter how they were translated, my goals shifted immediately.

But guess what. He was the pastor; I worked to support his ministry. He could rearrange my work goals anytime he wanted—so can my current pastors! I've found out through the years it's more fun to work for someone who has a vision for growth and wants to build the kingdom of God.

When you work for a leader who has a vision for excellence and growth, you won't get bored. You'll hear yourself pray what I pray daily and have been praying for years: "Lord, just let me keep up and lead in new ways. Give me what's needed for my next level."

I know establishing your roles, priorities, and goals takes effort. But if you're clear on them, you can be effective in your work.

You see, you can be very busy in doing ministry work and still not accomplish a blessed thing. *Don't mistake activity for making progress.* Being busy isn't a virtue—you've got to be busy doing the right things.

Post your list of top priorities where you'll see it often. When you look at your priorities, ask yourself which ones need immediate attention, which ones are long-range goals and can take some time for action, and which ones may no longer be relevant. As your children grow older and leave home, your "parent with excellence" priority and goals will certainly change. Other priorities will shift too.

As an example, let me share a list of my roles and priorities. I also have goals that fit under my priorities, but that list is too long to include.

1. Follower of Jesus Christ

   - I will follow, worship, obey, and love God.

2. Husband

   - I will be a faithful husband to Julie, and I will be a loving man she's proud to have as a husband.

3. Father and Grandfather

   - I will be a father who models and instills God's principles in the lives of Yancy and Whitney and their husbands; I will be a support and guide in their development of passing faith to Sparrow, Rhythm, and Royal.

4. Executive Operations Pastor

   - I'll help my pastors, Henry and Alex Seeley, to implement their God-given vision for The Belonging Co. I'll be a faithful servant and an excellent staff member.

   - I'll reflect the Lord's heart, as expressed in Matthew 12:47-50, to those I lead, who I will coach, care for, and confront, ever seeking to encourage each ministry I'm responsible for to excellence.

   - I'll champion the following ministry goals:

     - *Corporate*: I will enthusiastically embrace the church's vision statement and heart, as well as, steward the presence of God.

     - *Departments*: I will manage and mold the Operations Department including Finance, Business, Facilities, Security, IT, Database, Children's Ministry, and Guest Services to support and advance the church's heart in each of these areas.

     - *Individual*: I will perform my duties with excellence and continually grow in my skills.

- *Personal*:

  - I will be a man of God in every part of my life.

  - I will love and do the Word of God.

  - I will be a godly husband.

  - I will be a loving father and grandfather.

  - I will be an able minister and lover of people.

  - I will be a leaders' leader in word and example.

  - I will help those in my care to fulfill God's callings on their lives.

  - I will be healthy and in good physical condition.

  - I will be a soul winner.

  - I will continue to train and encourage other leaders through annual seminars, conferences, podcasts, and webinars.

  - I will provide helpful, anointed, quality resources for the next generation of ministry leaders, including books, podcasts, and teaching videos.

  - I will personally coach and mentor leaders who can and will become better leaders than I am.

CHAPTER 8:
MAINTAINING YOUR INTEGRITY

Being a leader isn't the same thing as being a politician. There are politicians who never quite tell you what they're going to do. Or they tell you what you want to hear. You learn right quick that their promises don't mean much.

That approach to working with people may get someone elected, but it doesn't make you an effective leader in the church. Ministry leaders need to have integrity to line up with God's Word and to do what they say they'll do. It's essential, but it's not always the way people in leadership do business.

Lying (and let's call this a *lack of integrity*—what it really is) can smooth out a rough situation. It can help you avoid conflict. It can oil a squeaky wheel. And it can also become a habit that destroys your character and ministry.

Do this: Listen to yourself for the next few days. Are you in the habit of telling people only what they want to hear? Leaving out key facts? Slanting the truth? Has that habit of compromise gotten a hold of you?

Are you authentic—the same person when you're with church people as you are when you're alone or off on a business trip? Does your leadership depend on people not knowing what you truly believe? Not knowing what you look at when you're flipping through the cable channels or surfing the web? If so, repent, my friend. Talk to the Lord about it, and also talk to your pastor or another trusted person. Give your heart and habits to God. Get your own house in order before trying to lead others.

Don't think you're fooling people. You may get along for a while, but they'll figure you out. And God knows all along. And you know who else is quick to spot a phony? Children.

I learned a long time ago that if I promise *children* something, I'd better deliver. That's why I hate outdoor activities in the ministry—I can't control the weather. It takes just one good thunderstorm to cancel a picnic, parade, or family movie night.

Here's an example of how making a promise got me in a *lot* of trouble:

We decided to drop Easter eggs in a field behind our church building back at church number three. Granted, they were not real Easter eggs; instead we bought seventeen thousand individually wrapped marshmallow eggs. We chartered a helicopter to lob the eggs down on the thousands of kids I was sure would show up for this event.

The field in the back of our building was bordered on one side by a subdivision, by a horse pasture on the opposite side, and on the third side by a huge oak tree.

We advertised for weeks. On the day of the event, the field was full of kids. It was also full of gusting wind courtesy of an approaching storm. I received word that the helicopter was grounded at the airport.

Two thousand kids, seventeen thousand Easter eggs, and no way to get them together. I had a problem.

What could I do? I'd promised an egg drop, so I had to deliver one—no matter what.

The pilot scratched his head and offered to instead fly a small plane he owned. The plane wasn't grounded, even with high winds in the area. The pilot couldn't make a precise drop, but if he made a couple passes to calculate the drift of the eggs, and if his brother hung out the door to lob the eggs—it might work.

What choice did I have?

I agreed, and within thirty minutes, a tiny plane sputtered into view over the field of upturned grinning faces.

On the first pass, the pilot's brother emptied a box of eggs out of the door, and the eggs caught a wind gust. Over in the subdivision, eggs landed everywhere—on cars, on roofs, and in yards. People exploded out of their houses to find out why they were under attack.

During the second pass as the plane flew low, the horses decided they were under attack. They went berserk, ripping back and forth, wild-eyed and frantic. But the eggs hit the target. Kids were scrambling for eggs!

But that's when someone pointed at the plane. Apparently, the pilot was concentrating so hard on the egg drop that he'd forgotten about the big oak tree.

He was headed straight toward it with his brother pointing frantically while hanging out of the door.

The good news: The pilot missed the tree . . . by inches.

The bad news: Between frustrated neighbors and an irate horse owner, the Federal Aviation Administration got so many phone calls that they pulled the pilot's license for a time. And our neighbors weren't too thrilled with us either.

I'd kept my promise to the kids but at a high, high price. I'd have been smarter to schedule something that didn't require blue skies and mild weather.

Integrity requires we keep our promises—that the children and adults we serve know that we mean what we say and do what we promise to do. But even beyond that, integrity demands we be authentic, including a willingness to admit when we've made mistakes.

Integrity isn't always easy.

Consider Joseph. In Genesis 39:41, we read about a guy who, after a rough start, was doing all the right stuff. He was living with integrity, but just the same, he got in trouble.

Joseph worked his way into a position of authority and then was tempted to commit adultery. When he refused, he ended up in prison.

Joseph had every earthly right to be bitter. He'd done the right thing—and look where it got him! But Joseph praised God, so he saw God's hand in what had happened. That was another piece of his integrity—Joseph worshiped God all of the time, not just when things went well.

I believe there are lots of reasons leaders fail, and at the core, many of them involve a lack of integrity. I'm not just talking about outright lying on a resume or falling into sexual sin. I'm talking about cutting corners, about sliding into a habit you wouldn't want your leaders to know about, about entertaining thoughts that fall way short of honoring God.

Remember, no ministry leader sets out to fail. But again and again, leaders who start out strong, crash and burn. After a few years, they're out of the ministry. Or they're still in ministry, but they're no longer leading.

What happened? And how can you keep it from happening to you?

I think it comes down to standing firm when you're tempted to set aside your integrity.

Temptations don't go away because you move into leadership. If anything, the devil attacks you with even greater intensity when you're a leader. That means you, friend, are under attack. You'd better be praying and asking others to pray for you too.

If you're like most leaders I've met, you're not immune to the following "integrity temptations." They are there every day, so every day you need to ask God for strength to turn to Him instead of elsewhere.

How are you doing with the following temptations?

THE TEMPTATION TO BE SELF-SUFFICIENT

We get a few years of ministry under our belt and decide we've got this ministry thing nailed. We read through the Bible or get our Bible degree, so we think we know it all. We pray at meals but let our personal devotion time slip. We start thinking God doesn't have anything more to tell us.

We start walking in our own power, thinking that being successful is better than being faithful. We're such good planners that we forget to ask God what He wants us to do.

If you're a Christian leader, you'll never be self-sufficient. Never. Not for one day. You are where you are to serve God and do what He wants done. If you're in leadership for any other reason, move aside or repent.

Integrity demands that you see yourself as God's servant—relying on Him all of the time, not just when people are watching.

THE TEMPTATION TO BE LAZY

We begin telling ourselves, "I've paid my dues. I've worked long and hard, so now I'll coast a bit."

We lose our passion. We lose our first love. We lose focus. We become caretakers, not leaders. We're like those pastors who just rotate through old sermons they've used in other places. We're not doing anything new or pushing for the change God wants to see in us and in our ministry.

Have you become lazy or complacent in your work? Are you excited or bored? Faithful or fading? When you encourage others to do their best for the Lord, are you speaking with integrity?

THE TEMPTATION TO COMPROMISE ON MORAL ISSUES

Things that were once black and white become gray. We once had ministry friends who honestly knew us, but we don't meet with them anymore. We aren't transparent with our mentors or our pastor any longer. We know we're hiding something.

It's not that we've gone out and murdered anyone, but we've taken the first few steps toward becoming someone who we don't respect. And the thought of taking the next few steps doesn't seem so bad.

Are you lying to yourself? Avoiding certain subjects when you talk to God? Avoiding time alone with God? Do you have a godly friend who knows you thoroughly—who knows even the stuff you don't want anyone else to know? Who? Have you given this person permission to speak truth into your life? Are you listening?

The devil doesn't need to persuade you to do something horrible to know you and your leadership are off track. All the devil needs to do is help you do something that causes you to feel shame. Once that happens, you'll pull yourself out of the game and set yourself on the bench where you're no good as a leader.

Do you feel shame about anything? Deal with it before God and a friend who loves both you and God, and arrange to spend regular time with that friend. Let that friend share with you the reassuring words God wants you to hear.

THE TEMPTATION TO LEAVE YOUR CALLING AND CHURCH

Has God called you to ministry? To minister in the spot you've serving right now? If so, why are you considering leaving or quitting just because things are tough?

I'll never forget the time at church number three when a little girl spotted the senior pastor and me walking down a hall. Her eyes lit up, and she yelled, "Pastor!" as she came running down the hall. My senior pastor leaned down and opened his arms, but she zipped right past him to give me a hug.

My pastor looked up at me and grinned. "Well, I guess I know where *I* stand," he said.

It could have been a terrible moment, but a little later he said to me, "I'm so proud of the relationship you have with the boys and girls in this congregation." He understood how to love people, and he was willing to share the limelight with me.

That's the sort of pastor you want to serve under. A pastor who values serving all ages —who values you. When you find a pastor like that, it's a joy to serve them.

But what if that's not the spot you're in right now?

I remember back at my first church, we'd grown from a handful of kids to a crowd of three hundred children. As I prayed about what direction to head next, I received a vision about my ministry. I saw myself equipping leaders and influencing churches.

I asked the senior pastor for a meeting so I could bring him up to date. It turned out he also wanted to meet with me.

He started by leading me on a walk around the church property. He pointed out where he saw new buildings going up on the campus to support new ministries. And he said, "You know, I never really wanted the children's ministry to get this big. I'd like you to focus more on adult ministry, and quit spending so much time with the kids. And someday when I retire, well, I think maybe you'll be ready to be the senior pastor."

I was stunned. When he turned to me and said, "Now, what was on your mind?" my answer came out as a surprise, even to me.

"I think it's time for me to leave," I said.

I'd assumed that the new level of leadership and serving God called me to would happen at that church. I was rock-solid certain I was supposed to labor in the field of children's ministry. And that meant I couldn't shift my focus as my pastor had requested.

I believe you work for the pastor. It's your job to find out what the pastor wants and to deliver it. But if God's specific call on your life won't let you follow your pastor's vision for ministry or leadership, then step aside so someone else can fill your spot, even if you aren't sure where you'll go next.

Look, ministry is hard. There are people who will not embrace or follow you no matter what you say or do. There are situations that will grind you down if you let them. There are problems that are beyond your control to fix.

Believe it or not, sometimes the people who challenge your leadership most don't do it because of you. It's nothing personal. They're trying to get at your pastor through you. Or they don't think a particular ministry should get so much attention and support. Or they're mad about something totally unrelated to you or your ministry, and you're just in the line of fire.

But God is still God. He's still with you. And He's still good all the time—no matter how you feel, no matter what you've done—or are considering doing—He's calling you back into a close walk with Him.

So are you on track or derailed? What are you going to do about it?!

CHAPTER 9: DELEGATION

I was audited by the Internal Revenue Service back at church number two.

It wasn't all that bad. I won my auditor to the Lord, which made the experience worthwhile all by itself, and, as a bonus, I found out what other people think we do as children's ministry leaders.

While the auditor could understand me wanting to write off a new Bible—that made sense; he had a harder time with clown makeup, balloons, food for kids, and more. What did those things have to do with children's ministry?

It took some explaining on my part. Ministering to kids involves stuff, *lots* of stuff. Stuff to snag kids' attention, to illustrate Bible points, and to entertain them while you're sharing the Gospel.

And food? I thought everyone knew the cardinal rule of ministry to kids and youth: If you feed them, they will come. The IRS wasn't familiar with that concept, but I've straightened them out. You can thank me for it if you ever get audited yourself.

The fact is that working with children takes a lot of skills. You've got to be a teacher, a preacher, and it helps if you're also a musician. You should know your way around a few illusionist tricks, too, and it doesn't hurt to have some stand-up comic skills. A degree from clown college isn't a bad idea, and you'd better be up to speed in drama, mime, ventriloquism, cartooning, storytelling, arts and crafts, and full bodied costumes.

No wonder you're tired!

Oh, and you also need to be an expert in visitation and pastoral care, advertising and social media marketing, and be a liaison with social agencies in your community. You've got to know the law as it relates to the next generation and families. And then there's dealing with audio and video and photography. These days you're sunk without computer and graphic-design skills too.

And you'll likely organize a summer camp or a cross-cultural ministry in your church, and then you can add another two pages of skills necessary onto this list. You'll handle situations and people that would make a sociologist or psychologist call for backup.

And, friend, that's just dealing with the day-to-day. If you attend board meetings, you'd best also be a diplomat, accountant, and a business expert.

Plus, over half of your ministry isn't to just the age group you work with at all—it's to adults too. You've got the kids' parents, the adults on your ministry staff, the volunteers, other folks on staff at the church, not to mention the level of leadership above you.

Feeling overloaded yet?

Many of us went into children's ministry because we wanted to spend all of our time ministering to kids. That's not the reality of the situation. If you don't learn how to motivate and rally adults in ministry and how to train and delegate, you'll fail. You have to master those skills too.

There's no way you can do everything yourself. You can try, but it won't work no matter how many hours you put in.

Here's the good news: you're not *supposed* to do everything yourself.

Read Ephesians 4:11-12 again. Remember, God gave some to be pastors and teachers, not so they could shoulder specific ministry program themselves, but so they could equip others for service.

Effective leaders don't let themselves burn out doing everything themselves. They help others become effective in doing ministry. And that means you've got to stop doing it all yourself.

I see you nodding but then sighing. "Pastor Jim, you just don't understand. I've asked people to help me. I've *begged* people to help me. But these folks just won't do it. Since I'm the leader or director, they think it's my job to make things happen."

Well, those folks are wrong. The Bible says so, and you should say so too.

"But, Jim, if I get everyone else doing ministry, what will *I* do? People will think they don't need me anymore."

Listen, you'll always have work to do. Leaders have plenty to keep themselves busy if they're leading the way God wants his people led.

Exodus 18:20-21 records some great advice Moses' father-in-law gives Moses about dealing with the people of Israel: "Teach them His decrees and laws, and show them the way they are to live and how they are to behave. But select capable men from all the people—men who fear God, trustworthy men who hate dishonest gain—and appoint them as officials over thousands, hundreds, fifties, and tens."

You may not have thousands over which to appoint leadership yet, but I'll bet you've got ten. As a ministry leader, it's your job to find and equip those overseers and to shepherd them so they can shepherd others.

That's the job God has placed before you that only you can do. Others can set up chairs and hand out snacks or brew coffee. But only *you* can provide leadership to those who serve in the ministry you are responsible for.

So why are you spending all day designing a publication about small groups? Why are you straightening chairs after youth group? How come you're checking the battery in the wireless microphone? Couldn't someone else do it instead?

You can be so busy doing the work of ministry that you don't get around to doing ministry. You don't pray. You don't work with your leaders. You don't do the follow-up and vision casting that keeps your ministry moving forward.

Instead, you're running around looking for more crayons.

You must learn to delegate well. The alternative is ministry meltdown. Maybe not today or tomorrow but someday. You're planting the seeds of your own destruction if you can't delegate. It's that important.

Delegation isn't a dirty word. It's not sloughing off your work or treating others badly. It's not giving away the crummy jobs and keeping the good stuff for yourself.

In Genesis 1:28, God blesses mankind and says, "Be fruitful and increase in number; fill the earth and subdue it. Rule over the fish in the sea and birds in the sky and over every living creature that moves on the ground." That's delegation. God gave us the skills and resources to rule over creation—to be caretakers—and then handed us the responsibility and authority to do the job.

When you delegate well, you give away not just a task or a responsibility but the *authority* to get the job done. Delegation can be fulfilling, not just for the person handing out the jobs but for the person who's been entrusted with a job.

Effective leaders delegate.

Here are nine steps to mastering delegation. Like most leadership skills, it begins not with how you do it but with who you are.

1. FIGURE OUT WHY YOU'RE DOING EVERYTHING YOURSELF.

Have a little chat with yourself and the Lord. Exactly why are you so overwhelmed? Answering that question tells you a lot about yourself and your ministry.

Perhaps it's because people expect too much of you. Get out your job description. Is it written anywhere, "Do everything that everybody expects, no matter how much and how long it takes?" If not, that means you can set reasonable boundaries.

Talk with your leaders. Point out everything on the job description you're expected to do, and be honest about your struggles to get it all done. Ask for help deciding which things to quit doing.

Perhaps it's because you expect too much of yourself. If you've ever heard yourself say, "What would they do without me around here?" you're in trouble. The fact is that important people die every day, and the world doesn't screech to a halt. If you got hit by a truck this week, the Lord would find a way to get the important things done without you next week.

What To Do If Your Job Description Is Either Nonexistent Or Totally Unreasonable

1. Write a job description—or rewrite one that's too vague or too big—and then run it by your leadership to make sure it's what they want.

2. If it's still unreasonable—and damages your health or relationship with your family because of performance expectation—ask God if He really has

called you to help this pastor. If yes, stay and move to step three. If no, leave.

3. Build a team to get everything in the job description done but not all done by you.

4. Raise your leadership to the next level.

5. Do step four again. Keep doing it.

Never quit learning and growing. It's up to you to make the unreasonable reasonable.

If you're trying to earn the Lord's favor, or people's favor, by being a workaholic, repent now. If you can't feel good about yourself unless your big Christmas event goes off without a hitch, lighten up. The wings will always fall off an angel or the donkey will wander down the aisle, or Mary will drop the baby Jesus doll. People expect it. They even *enjoy* it.

My point is that you're not perfect. The Lord knows it; people know it; so it's important you realize that nobody expects it. Nobody but you, that is.

Perhaps you think nobody can do all things quite as well as you can. You're probably right. When you delegate a task, sometimes the quality slips a bit. You can overcome that by providing good training, but even then the person who leads for you may not do it as well as you can . . . at first.

My point is that you're not perfect. The Lord knows it; people know it; so it's important you realize that nobody expects it. Nobody but you, that is.

Perhaps you think nobody can do all things quite as well as you can. You're probably right. When you delegate a task, sometimes the quality slips a bit. You can overcome that by providing good training, but even then the person who leads for you may not do it as well as you can . . . at first.

Think about it. How did you develop your skills? Probably by someone letting you sorry all over a bunch of folks until you got better at leading.

Do this for me—and for yourself: Make sure the problem isn't your pride. I've known ministry workers who take so much ownership of their ideas or programs that they can't turn their proverbial babies over to others. These folks refuse to delegate. They're like jealous parents, and they drive away the help they need.

Perhaps you're running ahead of God's timing. You believe God wants you to launch an after-school tutoring program to reach hundreds of elementary latchkey kids, but you can't get enough adults to the building by 3:30 each day to get the program off the ground.

Consider starting small, and let God bring the resources you need to implement your larger vision.

If you're doing everything yourself, your first task is to fix that situation. Why? Because over time, the ministry will crumble. You will have failed to build a strong foundation.

2. IDENTIFY AND DEVELOP THE SKILLS YOU NEED TO DELEGATE EFFECTIVELY.

You can't delegate a job you can't define, so you'd better learn to write job descriptions (Chapter 12). People aren't going to take on jobs until they understand the scope of what you're asking them to do.

And while you're at it, you'd better master the technology available to you.

I remember my first computer. People told me it would save me time and help organize our ministry, but for the first few days, I sure couldn't see it. All I did was type. I didn't talk to people, visit others, or write lessons. I built databases.

"Great," I thought, "I'm further behind now than I've ever been."

But then I hit the "sort" button, and stuff that had been impossible to find appeared in alphabetical order. I could delegate tasks because, at last, I could give people the information they needed to be successful.

If you find yourself saying, "It's easier for me to do it myself" because you don't know how to put together a spreadsheet, *learn to put together spreadsheets.* Someone in your church can show you.

Don't let a lack of skills (budgeting, planning, recruiting, etc.) get in the way of being able to delegate tasks. It's worth learning what you need to learn—you'll recover your investment of time many times over.

3. GET GOOD AT WHAT YOU DO SO YOU CAN TRAIN OTHERS.

Confession—I'm not the best person to be doing everything in my job description. For instance, I'm not the guy you want designing a publication or coming up with creative copy. But I can do it well enough to explain to a graphics person and communicate to writers what needs doing—and why.

You don't need to be an expert in every ministry area to delegate the tasks of every ministry. But you do need to be able to communicate to others what they should accomplish, and you will have to provide the resources and leadership they need to be successful.

Remember, you can't delegate to people who aren't following you. You earn the option of delegating when you earn the respect of your followers.

4. BE READY TO DELEGATE.

You want to know why next week the Lord won't send you one hundred volunteers, each one wanting to help out in your ministry? Because if they did come, you wouldn't be able to put them to work.

Until you know what you'll do with volunteers—which jobs they'll do, how they'll be trained, and when they'll start—don't expect God to send them to you.

Be ready to qualify volunteers God sends by identifying their gifts. Not everyone who wants to help you can do so. Some people are just not cut out to work in every ministry.

If someone thinks kids should be seen and not heard, that's not a hot candidate for your children's ministry. Neither is someone who just wants to play games and who describes himself as a "big kid."

The world is full of people who are loving and sweet, but they simply have no business discipling young people. They lack the aptitude or gifts. No amount of study will overcome a teacher's inability to put up with wiggles and giggles down in the preschool room. If God designed someone to require order and quiet with a place for everything and everything in its place, children's ministry is not for that person.

So don't place those people in your ministry, and don't delegate responsibility to them. They are a better fit someplace else. You don't want a person in the wrong ministry; they won't stick.

How do you determine a person's giftedness? There are plenty of surveys and tests available, but I've found that gifts tend to track along with what people do well, enjoy doing, and find fulfilling. So long as those things glorify God and build up the church, I suspect they're working within their spiritual giftedness. And the way to confirm that is to actually get folks into appropriate areas of service, and see how they take to it.

5. EQUIP OTHERS TO HELP YOU.

Even when God sends the right people, you've got to train them before you can delegate tasks to them.

Be wise about training. Pour yourself into increasing the skills of the people on your team, but do it in the right way.

Training isn't verbal; it is *modeling*. It's letting a learner come alongside someone who already knows how to do it. There's time to watch, time to ask questions, time to try things and get immediate, informed feedback.

If you think training is just a matter of tossing a book at new teachers or having them sit through a few classes, may the Lord save your students . . . and your teachers. It's not going to be pretty.

You cannot successfully delegate tasks to people who are unprepared to receive them. That's like having a football quarterback toss the ball down-field to the team mascot instead of a receiver. It's just not going to work.

What's your training program and on-boarding look like? If it's not the admiration of your ministry buddies, make it that way. And making it that way is as easy as asking your very best workers to mentor new workers.

6. DELEGATE AND THEN RELEASE.

Start by getting people trained, then delegating an assignment consistent with each volunteer's gifting. Then allow your volunteers to do ministry in their own unique ways.

You've got to do two things at the same time—make a delegated job both incredibly simple but not boring.

Here's what I mean. Suppose you've got a worship leader who wants to lead worship in youth. You'll want to make sure she's good with students and that she understands how to worship. You'll want to make sure she selects songs that fit your ministry and your kids. There's a lot you'll want to spell out so that she is effective.

But you've also got to let her have some room to express herself. Nobody wants to volunteer for a job that's so structured it's boring. If she's going to grow in that role, there's got to be room for her to grow.

And another thing—you've got to be willing to delegate some of the fun jobs you'd rather do yourself. I happen to love leading worship in kids' church, but years ago I learned that I've got to be a big enough leader to let someone else take that role.

Is there a job you've hung onto that someone else could do? If you delegated that job, what could you do with the time and energy it frees up?

7. EVALUATE.

When you delegate a task, that doesn't mean you're done with it forever. You've got to follow up and check on the outcome.

People won't always tell you if they need more training or if the task isn't going well. They may not even know they're in trouble until it's too late. If it's the first time they're ever done the job, they may miss the danger signs.

Go inspect. Make mid-course corrections. Encourage. Empower. Confront. Find out if there are problems, and fix them.

8. KEEP COMMUNICATING YOUR VISION.

The people who have already responded to you and your vision, and to whom you've already delegated tasks, still need to hear from you.

In fact, they may need to hear from you more that the people who haven't yet responded to your invitation to come do ministry with others. Now that they've taught classes or stuffed envelopes or poured lemonade awhile, the "shine" may have worn off the job.

We sometimes forget about the old-faithful worker who we have worked alongside forever. That's an expensive mistake. You want to keep those precious people on board, so keep the vision in front of them. Coach them. Ask them if they're ready to handle more responsibility or if they want to move to another job that also serves the Lord and helps reach the vision for your ministry.

9. GIVE CREDIT WHERE CREDIT IS DUE.

If you've delegated preparing something to Sarah, one of your leaders, and your leader compliments you on Sarah's creation, pass that compliment along to Sarah. And make sure your leader knows it was her work. Ask your leader to thank her personally.

Become a cheerleader for your team, and you'll find that other people will want to join the team. It's just natural.

Give credit to God too. Don't think for a moment that growth in your ministry is only due to you. It's all about you following God's plan, and God using you.

Get a reputation for humility, for sharing the glory, and for integrity. Earn a reputation like that, and you'll find people far more willing to take on tasks you need to delegate.

Finally, keep in mind that the more skills you build as a leader, the better you'll be able to delegate. The next few chapters will help you master the use of key leadership skills so you can add them to your "leader toolbox."

CHAPTER 10:
PROBLEM SOLVING

Want to test the measure of a leader? Throw a problem at him or her.

When most people come face to face with problems, they immediately look for others to solve them. We all start out that way. As children, when problems come our way, we call for our mamas. And that is completely appropriate for children but not for a leader. It's a follower mentality.

Leaders respond differently when facing a problem. They act to solve it. Those sorts of people are like Daniel: "Daniel, whom the king called Belteshazzar, was found to have a keen mind and knowledge and understanding, and also the ability to interpret dreams, explain riddles, and solve difficult problems" (Daniel 5:12). Daniel had a reputation for being able to solve problems. It's a reputation you want to earn too.

But before we talk about how to solve problems, there are a couple of things you need to know about problems.

Not all problems are bad.

I often hear ministry workers wish they lived problem-free lives.

Well, there are people who have a problem-free existence, but they're all dead. The only people I know who don't have to deal with challenges like stress, budgets, and relationships are stretched out in the cemetery.

Notice, I said *challenges* rather than *problems*; that's no accident. I've found that some things I consider problems turned out to be tremendous blessings. They're the very situations that helped me grow and changed my life for the better.

Whatever problems you face in ministry, decide to view them not just as problems but also challenges Holy Spirit wants to help guide you through. That attitude keeps you teachable, and it invites divine guidance.

You may look back at the problems in your life right now and thank God for them because they caused you to grow. Here's why.

Some problems prepare you to handle more.

Problems season you and prepare you for more responsibility.

When David walked out to face Goliath, it wasn't the first time he'd fought a larger enemy. He'd already bested a lion and a bear. Goliath might be carrying a spear, but David knew he could place a rock in just the right place to drop the giant. David had faced down big, hairy problems before.

Think about your life. How many of the problems you've faced were just training—warm-ups that prepared you for larger problems that followed?

Some problems are learning opportunities.

I remember the day at church number one when we decided to start a puppet ministry. I'd never held a puppet before, but my roommate was on a college puppet team.

He walked us through what we needed to know. And I took *really* good notes because the next week I was going to be in charge. I went from absolute ignoramus to Mr. Director in one week—quite a transformation! But that ministry was successful.

If I'd seen my lack of experience as a problem, it would have stopped me cold. Instead, I saw it as a challenge, and in the process of overcoming it, I learned some new skills. Even today, I know the same God who helped me learn puppet ministry will guide me through mastering electronics.

What current challenges are teaching you something new? Like it or not, you've got to be a problem solver. People who serve under you already see you as a problem solver, so they need you to take on that role.

For most of us in ministry, problem solving isn't our strongest skill. We're wired to be caretakers. We love feeding the sheep God's entrusted to us. We're natural-born teachers. We're not so good at doing the administrative analysis, measuring, and evaluation that help us solve problems *before* they develop into full-blown crises.

Does the notion that people expect you to solve problems make you uncomfortable? If so, you're in good company. There's a long list of outstanding leaders in Scripture who failed as problem solvers.

When the people told Moses they needed water, Moses smacked a rock with a stick, which disappointed God. Daniel fell short now and then in the problem-solving department. Peter wanted to do something to help out Jesus in the Garden of Gethsemane, so he drew a sword and lopped off someone's ear.

Being a problem solver doesn't mean you always have the right answer at your fingertips or that you always make the right decision or do the right thing. But it does mean you're willing to make a decision and face problems head on.

Do you think of yourself as a problem solver?

PROBLEM SOLVERS' CHARACTERISTICS

I've learned from some excellent problem solvers, and here are some characteristics they display when it's time to toss rocks at their Goliaths.

Problem solvers are willing to give it a try.

If you walk often enough past a fence that needs to be painted, you'll quit noticing that the paint is peeling. You get used to the problem. And when you get used to problems, they quit feeling like problems. You no longer feel an urgency to roll up your sleeves and try to fix things.

Leaders identify challenges as challenges—and they act. *They think of themselves as problem solvers.* They're proactive and intentional in making things better.

What's your approach when a challenge finds you? Do you turn and face it? Or do you ignore it, hoping it will go away?

Problem solvers explore options.

A friend of mine has been calling me for years now, and he always says, "I think God's calling me to leave this church and go to another church." Then he lists all the challenges he's currently facing.

So I ask, "Why don't you get out of there? If God's calling you somewhere else, quit so you're ready to move forward."

That's when he backpedals, "Well, then I'd just be facing a whole new set of problems. At least here I know what they are."

He's right. He will find new challenges wherever he goes—that's life. But if God's calling him to move, God will help him deal with the challenges he runs into down the road. My friend just isn't willing to explore new opportunities. He's stuck.

We get stuck too. Maybe it's fear or apathy or just being worn out, but sometimes when our first try to solve a problem doesn't work, we surrender.

But the first solution often isn't the best solution. Best solutions are often the third or fourth . . . or twentieth idea that comes to mind when you're figuring out how to get through or around a challenge.

How quickly do you stop at your first solution? How well do you explore options?

Problem solvers seek the advice of others.

I remember decades ago trying to put a swing set together for my daughters. The instructions made no sense to me, so I found someone who'd put a swing set together for his kids. He told me he'd made a complete mess of the entire thing.

That's the guy I asked to come on over. As he described what he'd done, I did the opposite, and the project came together.

Effective problem solvers don't necessarily look for advice from the smartest person they know. They look for someone who's tackled the problem. Even if that person failed, you can learn something. And notice that good problem solvers aren't afraid to ask for advice. They're open to new information. They're willing to admit that they don't have all the answers.

Will you admit it when you don't know? Will you ask for advice?

Problem solvers take reasonable risks.

There are risks involved in everything. But there are risks, and there are *risks*. Not every risk is worth taking.

Reasonable risks include things that don't jeopardize your health or the lives of people you serve. They don't create total chaos and confusion in your ministry. They don't have people questioning your salvation or your sanity.

But they do include trying new things, stretching yourself.

If God clearly tells you to do something, that's no risk at all—no matter how strange it might sound. When God told Noah to take up boat building, it had to sound like the craziest thing anyone had ever heard . . . until the rain started to fall.

You'll never step out and be the leader God wants you to be without taking risks. Are you willing?

Problem solvers pray.

I know people who when they face a problem, frantically try one solution after another; and then when all else fails, they pray.

That's backward.

Listen, if you're leading in the church, you need to be a person of prayer. If you lead by sight alone, you're headed for a cliff, and you're leading everyone right along with you.

Pray about decisions and challenges *first*. Allow God to guide and use you. That's what He wants, and that's who you're working for.

TEN STRATEGIES FOR SOLVING PROBLEMS

As I've watched leaders I admire face challenges, I've taken notes. And over the years, I've put together a ten-step process that has served me well when challenges come my way. I'd suggest you use it too.

1. Listen for God's answer.

When I've gone to the Lord about a problem, He's clearly shown me what to do. So I did exactly what He said, and the problem was solved. "Thus saith the Lord" always works, remember?

But sometimes the Lord doesn't provide me with a clear answer. Maybe I'm not listening, but there are times I ask for guidance and hear nothing. So the problem is still sitting there.

Personally, I think the Lord doesn't care how you solve some problems, so long as your solution honors Him. The older I get, the more I see there are a lot of ways to do things. He leaves it up to you. He just wants you to solve the problem. He's given you permission.

When problems present themselves, do you pray? And do you listen for God's answer?

2. Identify the problem clearly.

When you face a challenge, figure out precisely which problem you're trying to solve, and I mean *precisely*. Get it down to one sentence that everyone involved can agree on. Otherwise, you'll spend a lot of time fixing the wrong stuff.

Back at church number four, as I walked down the hall between services, I saw a weeping woman standing by our elementary registration table—a *pregnant* weeping woman. A pregnant weeping woman holding a *form*.

The lady was sobbing, but what was the problem? Was it related to people at the registration table? Or was it a health difficulty related to her pregnancy? Had something happened during our ministry time that got her crying? Was there a problem with the form? Was her crying a good thing or a bad thing? Before I could help provide a solution, I had to figure out what was going on because I had absolutely no idea.

It turned out she had been handed a preschool form by accident, and the volunteer couldn't find the right elementary form to replace it. That's all. No big spiritual crisis.

The next day I realized the root issue wasn't the woman. We seldom had people breaking into tears at the registration table. But we did give out the wrong form, and there were fourteen separate steps to fix what went wrong—from initiating new policies and procedures (e.g., when you're at the registration table and run out of forms, who do you tell?), to keeping additional forms in a more accessible place (locking them in the church office wasn't the best idea), to having a box of tissues located nearby.

When you're faced with a challenge, do you take the time to make certain you know exactly what it is before you try to solve it?

3. Ask, "Why did this happen?"

It's not enough to identify a problem and find a solution for it. That's good, but you need to take it a step further. You've got to then discover *why* the problem happens.

I was out of town once when I got a message that the overhead door in our children's ministry area at church number four had come off the hinges. A repair company was fixing it. The problem was under control.

Well, almost.

In the middle of the week, when nobody was using that room, the door came unhinged again. It turned out that someone who was giving a tour of the facility didn't know how to operate the controls. Which meant if we left the key that operated the garage-door motor in the box with other keys, this could happen again during the next tour. Fixing the door was just *part* of the problem.

The good news is that there are plenty of problems and challenges to keep you busy. You don't have to face the same ones over and over. In fact, if that's happening, *you* are most likely the problem.

How faithful are you at digging to find out why a problem happens?

4. List ways to solve the problem.

Almost always there are many ways to solve any one problem. Some are good and some are bad but they're all possibilities. And you want to see them all before you throw any of them away. Choose the best, realizing that what's best today may change tomorrow.

At one church where I served, some very smart people decided the best way to provide music in the sanctuary was to install a pipe organ. It cost a fortune. Later, when sound systems came along, their decision didn't seem so smart—times had changed.

Don't get caught in the trap of thinking your best solutions for problems will always be best. Stay open to frequently making up new lists of possibilities.

Is your way always the best way? Is the first solution you tumble across the one you usually select? Are you open to changing that?

5. Identify factors that limit which decision you can make.

Maybe the best possible solution to your ongoing transportation problem is for your church to buy a church van. But with $18.74 in the church savings account, it's too expensive.

Maybe the week after your VBS crafts destroy the carpet isn't the time to ask for new computers. Timing can be everything.

Cost is often a limiting factor. So is effort. And church political considerations are always something to keep in mind. It may come as a shock, but politics can creep in at church.

What are the factors that matter in your church? Is it cost, effort, politics, timing, or other things? You'd better know because, like it or not, those factors determine, in part, how you go about solving problems.

6. Remember to consult history.

How has the problem been handled in the past? If you can keep from making the same mistakes your predecessor made, good for you. Ask some longtime volunteers what's been done before. Don't reinvent the wheel. And check around outside your church for insights too.

Years ago we decided to give our bus workers one Saturday a month off. It seemed okay to us, but we had never tried it. We had no idea what it would do to our program.

So I got on the phone and called around. I never did find a church who did that precise thing, but a church in New York gave its workers the entire summer off. So I peppered its staff members with questions: How did it affect the program? How eager were the workers to come back? How did it impact the kids? I learned from their history, and it helped me to proceed. It made a big difference.

7. Determine if this solution is an exception or sets a precedent.

When you give the okay once, you may be setting yourself up for making this the solution you always have to provide.

Suppose you absolutely cannot find volunteer nursery workers for a special service. So you call up some high school and college girls and one nursery supervisor, and you offer to pay them to cover the nursery.

Have you just set the expectation that during all special meetings you'll pay people to help? Unless you're clear this is a one-time exception, you've set a precedent you'll need to live with forever.

8. Ask yourself, "Do I feel good about my proposed solution?"

Does your solution have integrity? Will you be proud to raise your hand when someone asks where it came from?

It's tempting to shave corners or to take an easy way out to avoid conflict. But if you're considering a solution that doesn't maintain the highest standard of integrity, God won't let you feel peace about it. *Listen to Holy Spirit's voice, and obey the prompting.*

9. Consider your solution from another person's perspective.

Sometimes solving one problem creates other problems. And solving a problem in a way that makes sense to one person may confuse everyone else.

For instance, in an effort to be visitor friendly, you might post some "Visitor Parking Only" signs in the parking lot next to your building.

And for two Sundays nobody parks there. Nobody. Senior citizens who would appreciate parking close to the door are upset. Moms who lug in babies, diaper bags, and who knows what else are upset. And your visitors are still hiking in from the far side of the lot.

As a last step before implementing a problem-solving solution, ask, "How will it appear to others?" Does your solution cause more problems than it solves?

10. Put feet under your plan and then evaluate.

Once you've planned the work, work your plan, and see how it goes. You'll discover wrinkles you couldn't anticipate until you had actually rolled it out. Don't be disappointed when they appear; it's part of the process. Fix them.

Then ask if you were successful. Are you seeing the results you wanted? Don't skip this step—it's the payoff! It's where you see if it's time to start over.

DON'TS AND DOS IN PROBLEM SOLVING

Don't be afraid to say, "I don't know," "I'll look into it," or "I'll get back to you."

There are times you don't have all the facts or you need to check with your leaders or you simply aren't ready to make a decision. When you're in any of those spots, refuse to make a decision until you do your homework.

Just make sure that if you promise to get back to someone, you do so in a timely manner.

Don't allow yourself to be rushed.

Don't get pressured into making a decision too quickly.

In hospital emergency rooms, not all problems are equal. Limp in with a sore toe, and you'll get bumped back behind someone who arrives on two separate stretchers. The process is called *triage*, which is a fancy medical term for "deciding who needs help now, who can wait, and who is past help." Do triage with the ministries you oversee.

I walk down the hall at our church, and I can see twenty-eight things that need improving. I'd be a very frustrated man if I couldn't also see that twenty-six of those things aren't critical—they can wait. I really only have to get two of the things on my list fixed in the next week.

Don't ignore trends.

I'm a fanatic about checking attendance numbers, not just totals, but age groups and classes from week to week. I chart and compare numbers constantly.

I'm looking for developing trends in attendance and in budgeting. I know where we hit walls last year; I want to know if we're hitting the same walls this year. You see, if you're addressing the same problems you've addressed before, what you think is the problem isn't *really* the problem. Either you've fixed the wrong thing, or else you're just really bad at fixing that problem.

If every June you run out of money, you're not doing the right things with the information you've received. You've missed a predictable trend.

Don't wait for problems to manifest themselves before you fix them.

Look ahead. Ask yourself, "If we grow by 20 percent this year, how will our kids' classrooms handle the increase?" If you know that you'll need to make a change, then make that change now. You'll be ahead of the curve and ready for growth.

The perfect time to fix something is *before* it breaks.

And it's worth your time to develop a Plan B for situations that call for decisions. What if it rains? What if the power goes out? What if nobody shows up?

Don't focus on the problem once you've got a solution. Focus on the solution.

The Apostle Peter stepped out of a boat to walk on water to where Jesus stood. Bold move, especially for a fisherman who was familiar with the sea.

Peter didn't need to worry about waves. The solution for his buoyancy problem was right in front of him—Jesus. But Peter couldn't quite stop focusing on the waves; he took his eyes off Jesus, and that sunk him in a hurry.

We can learn something from Peter. When we've got a solution in sight, let's stay focused on it, not on the problem. As hard as it is to let go of the problem, it's essential. Otherwise we don't put our wholehearted energy into making the solution work.

If the solution is forgiving someone, do it and move on. I know people who still talk about problems they solved twenty years ago. The conflict flared up, was worked through and forgiven, but someone still remembers it and brings it up. That's not healthy . . . or Christian.

Don't keep doing what caused the problem in the first place.

My wife turned to me several years ago and said, "I want to learn to use a computer."

I couldn't believe it! I had bought lots of computers, but she had never wanted to even try using them. But then Julie realized that if our home-based business was going to increase, more than one person needed to be able to do the work, and all the work was done on the computer.

Julie understood that if we always do what we've always done, we'll always have what we've always had. Period. It's a law of nature, like gravity. The only way to break free and see new results is to make changes.

Something in your church or ministry allowed a problem to develop. Don't keep doing what it was that gave that problem the chance to form. Make changes.

Don't solve everyone's problems for them.

Leaders sometimes step in too quickly to solve problems. Then the person experiencing the problem doesn't get a chance to learn by fixing it.

If you want people who are serving with you in ministry to grow, ask them what they think they should do with a problem they bring to you. Give them the chance to solve it.

Don't fall in love with your past successes.

Okay, the idea worked in a church you use to serve, but what worked there may not work here. Be open to new ideas and approaches. The problem you face may only feel familiar; old solutions probably won't work.

Don't ever forget: Jesus lives inside you.

If God placed you in charge of a ministry or small group or classroom or section of the parking lot, that's not an accident. God is for you. No matter how tough your situation may be, remember God loves you and wants you to be successful in providing leadership.

You're not powerless. Your work is not wasted. You're not alone. Did I make my point?

The most important thing you can do with a problem is also the one thing that may frighten you the most: Confront it head on. Don't ignore it. Don't hope it goes away or gets better on its own.

You're a leader, and that means you're a problem solver. If now isn't the time to tackle the problem, when will be a better time?

See the next page for the top ten dos in effective problem solving.

THE TOP TEN DOS IN PROBLEM SOLVING

10. Do solve the problem—don't run from it.

9. Do solve the problem—don't run from it.

8. Do solve the problem—don't run from it.

7. Do solve the problem—don't run from it.

6. Do solve the problem—don't run from it.

5. Do solve the problem—don't run from it.

4. Do solve the problem—don't run from it.

3. Do solve the problem—don't run from it.

2. Do solve the problem—don't run from it.

1. Do solve the problem—don't run from it.

CHAPTER 11:
MAKING DIFFICULT DECISIONS

Here's the good news: God created you with the ability to make decisions. And here's the bad news: God created you with the ability to make decisions. As a leader you'll make lots of decisions. It's the ability to make difficult decisions that sets leaders apart from followers.

THE MOST IMPORTANT DECISION COMES FIRST.

Let me remind you of a familiar passage about making decisions.

In Joshua 23 and 24, we get to see a remarkable leader in action. Joshua gathers God's people together and reminds them of all God has done to deliver them from their enemies—and from themselves.

Then Joshua brings the history lesson to a clear decision: "But if serving the Lord seems undesirable to you, then choose for yourselves this day whom you will serve. But as for me and my household, we will serve the Lord" (Joshua 24:15).

Joshua knew each person listening could choose to serve, but no matter what anyone else did, Joshua intended to make the right choice. And when Israel's leader chose to follow God, that allowed God to let blessings flow through Joshua to the people who followed Joshua.

Joshua knew something that maybe you're just figuring out: The higher up in leadership you are, the tougher the decisions you'll face . . . and more people will be affected by your decisions.

Fortunately, most of the decisions I made as a teenager affected only me. When I made mistakes, I paid the price, dusted myself off, and moved on.

But when I got older and became a husband and father, my decisions affected not only me but also my wife and children. The impact of decisions I made had far greater consequences. And when I became a pastor, suddenly my decisions affected not just me, not just my family, but hundreds of families, thousands of people.

We all make poor decisions. What we do, how we act, what we say, there are plenty of opportunities to make bad calls. I know I've made my share.

At my first church, I led kids ministry without once thinking like a parent when I scheduled meetings and activities. I'm lucky those parents didn't hurt me. I made some horrible choices. If any of those parents are reading this, please accept my apology right here and now.

Decisions matter. Leaders win or lose based on how they choose. The first and most difficult decision you face forces you to decide whether you'll do things your way or listen to the Lord and do things His way. Joshua made that decision, and it set the tone for the rest of his decisions.

Of course, you'll do things God's way. You're a ministry leader, right?

But what about when you're thinking it's time for you to move to a new ministry because you just can't seem to get things in gear where you are? What about giving up old techniques and trying something new? What about choosing to live a life that wouldn't embarrass you if everyone knew your business?

I remember a time when I played for a Christian band. We were right on the edge of landing a record contract. It came at the same time I was also offered a full-time job doing ministry at a church . . . for fifty bucks a week.

That's right. Full time. A whopping fifty bucks a week. I was making more than that in the *band*. But after much prayer, I knew what God wanted for me—so I went to the church.

The proof of a good decision isn't how you feel about the decision. The proof is fruit that comes from your decision. Is your ministry bearing more fruit because you decided to add a new nursery room to divide the ages up or promoted a new person to lead your mom's group? Every decision brings fruit—sometimes good and sometimes bad.

"I WANT YOUR DECISION—NOW!"

Some decisions demand immediate attention. When a person is physically hurt on church property, you've got to act now. But there are other decisions that can, and should, wait.

Effective leaders don't always make quick decisions. If your facility is on fire, then a quick decision is called for. But unless flames are licking at your feet, you can probably take time to make a deliberate decision. It's best to delay if . . .

- **You're tired.** When I'm tired, I just can't get excited about anything. Everything seems like a bad idea. If you're the same when you're overwhelmed or exhausted, it's smart to say, "Let me get back to you on that."

- **You don't have enough information.** If a little alarm goes off in your head that maybe you'd better check with the pastor, the Operations Pastor, the Facilities Director, or someone else whose opinion will make a difference, don't make a decision yet. Make a few calls first.

- **You haven't heard from all the right people.** The toughest decision often involves managing people. Should you fire someone? (See "How to Fire a Volunteer" in Chapter 12.) Should you dive in and help two other leaders resolve a conflict? Before you make an uninformed decision, let everyone who needs to weigh in do so.

Now, some people procrastinate when it comes to making tough decisions. It's as if they're waiting for Jesus to come back so they don't have to make the hard calls at all. That doesn't work. You've got to make decisions.

Remember, *leaders are decision makers.* Leaders take responsibility for their decisions.

TAKING RESPONSIBILITY FOR DECISIONS

Many people make decisions, but not all those people will take responsibility for their decisions. And a willingness to make decisions and then own them is the difference between leaders and followers.

Followers blame others. It's always somebody else's fault or some unavoidable situation to blame. Followers make excuses; leaders don't. Leaders know the truth of this statement: *You can't explain your way out of something you behaved yourself into.*

If you said you'd schedule nursery workers and you didn't, don't make excuses. If you failed to prepare your Bible lesson and you let down the kids, don't try to explain how work went crazy and kept you from preparing. There may be valid reasons you couldn't follow through. Things do come up; that's life. But if you let those things become excuses, that's a follower mentality.

Leaders take responsibility for what they decide—and what they do.

There's a guy who was on my staff at church number four that I still respect to this day. When I corrected him, he never made excuses. He listened, made sure he understood, and then he said, "That mistake will never happen again." And it didn't. Instead, he pushed ahead and made a different mistake, which was fine by me! That's what I'm after even still today. If you're not making mistakes, you're not trying anything new. Make all the new mistakes you want, but take responsibility for them.

WHY LEADERS MAKE POOR DECISIONS

Here are six of the most common traps. Are you falling into any of them?

Trap 1: They succumb to fear.

In Matthew 25:14-30, we read a parable Jesus told about three servants who received talents from their boss. One got five talents, the next guy got two, and the third man got one talent. You know the story. The first and second guys did something with the money they received, and both of them earned a "well done" from their master.

In verse 18, we see the third man bury the money. Why? The answer is there in verses 24 and 25, "I knew that you are a hard man . . . . So I was *afraid*" (italics mine).

We almost always make poor decisions when we let fear guide us.

Trap 2: They rely on their own abilities and wisdom.

We all bring some experience to our leadership. We've developed abilities and accumulated some wisdom, and that's a plus. But it can also be a weakness.

You can get in trouble if you're trying to lead under your own steam. If all you've got going for you is what you bring to the task, you're in trouble.

Proverbs 3:5-8 says, "Trust in the Lord with all your heart and lean not on your own understanding; in all your ways submit to Him, and He will make your paths straight. Do not be wise in your own eyes; fear the Lord and shun evil. This will bring health to your body and nourishment to your bones."

Now, nobody needs to tell me I don't know it all. I first came to the Lord because I nearly killed myself so often during my first seventeen years of life. I knew I needed a savior. Nobody needed to convince me I'd made a mess of things. Leaning on my own understanding wasn't getting me anywhere.

If you want to make right decisions, lean on God's strength and wisdom. Before you make a decision, ask yourself, "What does God's Word say about it?"

Proverbs 14:12 says, "There is a way that appears to be right, but in the end it leads to death." There are a lot of things that seem right to us, but they aren't right. Our wisdom is limited; we can get things wrong even with good intentions.

If I'm relying on myself alone, I'm going to make poor decisions. I know it may sound trite, but I've got to ask you: How much time do you spend in prayer about decisions you're facing? Are you asking God for the wisdom you need? Are you inviting Holy Spirit to lead you to what Jesus wants?

Trap 3: They let emotions and feelings cloud their judgment.

When I was young, my strategy for conflict resolution was to get in the first lick. I'd come up to you, pick up a chair, and smack you upside the head. I'd hit you one time, hard and ferocious. That pretty well settled it. But when I became a Christian, someone pointed out I couldn't do that anymore. I had to talk about things and settle the conflict with words.

That was a hard transition. My emotions said, "Pick up a chair, and let it fly," but I knew better. So sometimes I'd stop the discussion and ask if I could get back to the person I was fighting with. I needed to calm down.

It's hard to make a good decision when you're wrapped up in your emotions. Second Corinthians 5:7 says, "We live by faith, not by sight." It's not what we think or feel or wish. It's what God says. That's where the good decisions are. If we make decisions based on our emotions, we're basing our decisions on the wrong thing.

Trap 4: They let themselves be pressured into making decisions.

Just because you're standing in my office wanting a decision doesn't mean I'll give you one, especially if I don't have an answer. It's tempting to tell people something just so they'll go away, but that's a great way to say something stupid that you'll have to live with.

Pressure closes down your thinking; it narrows your options. Pile on enough pressure, and it'll literally kill you. And pressure most certainly increases the likelihood that your decisions will be poor ones.

What causes pressure in your life? Is it a church board that's demanding results? An out-of-control schedule? Is it your attempts to double attendance—even if nobody else expects it? Pressure can sap your energy and siphon off your joy.

And, by the way, the source of that pressure is never the Lord.

"Come to Me, all you who are weary and burdened, and I will give you rest. Take My yoke upon you and learn from Me, for I am gentle and humble in heart, and you will find rest for your souls. For My yoke is easy and My burden is light" (Matthew 11:28-30). That says it all. You have plenty to do, but you don't have to do it alone. When you work with God, you won't be overwhelmed.

Trap 5: They do what others do rather than what God has called them to do.

"Thus saith the Lord" always works. Underline that. Highlight it. Copy it down, and hang it on a wall somewhere. Write it on your planning calendar. Those six words will give you success in ministry like nothing else.

Maybe it's crazy for me to say that since I do seminars, webinars, and all other sorts of -nars all over the world, but it's true. Nowhere in the Bible does it say that you should do as the seminar speaker does. What works for someone at one church (regardless of the size or fame) may be the worst possible thing for you to do at your church.

Write down all the speakers' ideas and learn from their experiences. But when you get home, put those notes in a folder. Before you do anything you wrote down, ask Jesus what you should do in His church. What does He want to do through you? Once you've got that straight, pull out the notes, and see if anything you wrote down will help you get there.

"Thus saith the Lord" *always* works. Remember, Jesus is your shepherd, you are His sheep, you know His voice. The voice of a stranger you will not hear (John 10)!

Trap 6: They don't really trust God.

There's a difference between knowing who God is and trusting Him. Psalm 37:3-6 says: "Trust in the Lord and do good; dwell in the land and enjoy safe pasture. Take delight in the Lord, and He will give you the desires of your heart. Commit your way to the Lord; trust in Him and He will do this: He will make your righteous reward shine like the dawn, your vindication like the noonday sun."

When you put your trust in the Lord, you act on what the Word of God says. If Scripture weighs in on a decision you need to make, take God at His Word, and do what He says.

When you ignore God's word, you make poor decisions.

KEYS TO MAKING GOOD DECISIONS

I've yet to meet someone who launched a string of disasters on purpose. But how do you avoid it? When you consider all the things that can go wrong, it's amazing any good decisions get made at all. Here is my advice on making good decisions.

Decide you'll make the best decision.

When you're faced with making a decision, almost always a solution will immediately spring to mind. That solution usually involves you doing what you've always done, but is it the best solution?

We're creatures of habit in church work. If something worked well once, we stick with it until something goes wrong or the Lord comes back.

When Julie and I first got married, I did the cooking throughout the week, and she fixed Sunday dinner. And that first Sunday we had meatloaf, not just meatloaf— *great* meatloaf! I loved it. It was about as good as a meatloaf gets.

The second Sunday, there it was again—meatloaf. Why mess with a good thing, right? Except, even a great meatloaf is still a meatloaf. I asked if maybe the next Sunday we could do something different, and Julie agreed.

The third Sunday we had meatloaf *balls*—little individual meatloaves, and the fourth Sunday we were back to meatloaf.

I finally asked Julie if she could cook anything else. She couldn't. "But I make meatloaf really well, don't I?" she asked.

I'm happy to report that her cooking skills have widened remarkably (and so has her husband), and now when meatloaf appears, I'm happy to see it. If you ever come over to my house to eat, call ahead and ask her to make it—see if it isn't the best meatloaf you've ever tasted.

But isn't that how it is for us in church work too? We have success once with a program, so we keep going back to it. We don't ask the hard question—is this the best thing we could do with this time, money, and energy?

When it's once again time to run a program you've done before, ask your leader, "I know we've always done it this way, but is there any reason you'd like to see it done differently?" Or grab a couple of your best people, put them in a room, and ask, "If we couldn't do it the way we've always done it, what would you do?"

Consider the timing.

Is this the best time to implement your decision? Can you dedicate sufficient time to see what's necessary for success to get done? Would this interfere with another important initiative that's already underway? Will this step on toes you can miss if you wait a week?

Making a good decision is just part of the deal. You've also got to implement it, and timing is everything.

Here's a nugget that cost me dearly to learn: *Making a great decision doesn't mean much if you present it poorly or at the wrong time.*

There are times I've been certain I heard from the Lord on an issue. I knew in my bones the answer I had was the best possible one. But because I presented it poorly—and at the wrong time—it wasn't considered as a solution.

Maybe you work for someone who needs to see graphs, charts, and timelines before giving the okay to move ahead. Fine. Make graphs, charts, and timelines. Or maybe you work for someone who has to think it was his or her idea before giving it serious consideration. Fine, let your boss think that it was his or her idea. Maybe the answer will be received better if it's presented by someone else. If necessary, give the idea away, and let someone else get credit. It doesn't matter as long as your ministry moves forward.

The important thing is that you heard God's direction, and you followed it. When you ask God for guidance in selecting the best answer, also ask for wisdom in how and when to present it to others.

Know God's Word.

God's Word renews your mind. Your thoughts won't always produce good decisions, but God's thoughts will. You need to be thinking God's thoughts, seeing situations through God's eyes. Psalm 119:7-14 sums it up well, especially verse 11, "I have hidden Your word in my heart that I might not sin against You."

Knowing and obeying God's Word will help you make good decisions beginning with not sinning against God.

Check decisions against your ministry's mission statement.

What's your ministry's mission statement? If a decision helps you flesh it out, it's probably a good decision. If a decision moves you away from your mission, it's probably a bad decision.

A clear ministry vision statement and clear goals make a lot of your decisions for you. Assuming you created them with the input and approval of your pastor and leadership, they're your marching orders.

But if you face a particularly tough decision, ask your pastor or supervisor for input. What decision will best serve your leader's purpose? You're here to serve your pastor, so the actions you take need to line up with your pastor's goals.

Want to make it really easy for your pastor? Type up a brief email outlining the issue, some options, and your recommendation. Then ask how your pastor wants it done. Busy people want options. (I've always liked multiple choice questions better than essay questions.)

Make decisions that line up with your priorities.

If your top ministry priority is outreach, don't decide to spend your time designing costumes for an Easter pageant that only church people attend. If developing a mentoring program is something God wants you to do, don't decide to open a soup kitchen at this time. It's not that soup kitchens and Easter pageants are bad things. They're good things. But they may not be the most important things you could be doing.

Clear priorities help you make good decisions.

Seek the counsel of wise and trusted friends.

This is easier said than done. When we're facing a difficult decision, we often want to find people who'll nod sympathetically while we hold a pity party. We don't really want counsel; we want an audience.

Proverbs 11:14 says, "For lack of guidance a nation falls, but victory is won through many advisers." That's great advice, but the point isn't to talk to as many people as possible. That'll tie you up forever, especially if you're just looking for sympathy.

When you ask for advice, don't limit yourself to people who'll sympathize with you. Rather, talk with people who might have answers. These people may not be your buddies because that's not the point. *They're people who have something to offer.*

And while you're at it, *ask for prayer support.* I've got people I talk with who almost never have answers, but they are prayer warriors. They pray for me as I wrestle through hard decisions. Every leader needs intercessors. We all need a prayer covering.

Now is the time to identify wise people in your life who you can recruit as prayer warriors. Do it now, when there's no crisis to fix.

Check your church's policies and procedures.

I am in the middle of updating and coming up with a new employee manual at my church. It's not just for new hires. I'm expecting all employees to use it, even those who have been at the church for years. I'm expecting all of them to take time to read it from cover to cover, especially managers! Those expected to enforce it better know what's in it.

When's the last time you read your church's policy manual? That's assuming you've got one, of course. If you don't, create one. How do things get done around your place? Who cuts the checks? What's the budget procedure? What's the procedure when you realize the budget that got approved isn't going to last past October?

You're probably not the first person to tackle whatever decision is facing you. How has it been handled in the past? The answer may already be in print.

If it's not written down, check to see how the youth department handles similar issues. Or the children's ministry in *another* church you respect. And document how you solve a problem as you go through it. Why? Because you'll want to include that procedure in your next manual.

Decide how much change will be required.

Change isn't bad, but it can be uncomfortable. Before you make a decision that requires change, count the cost. What will it require of you? Of others? Of your organization?

If the change affects others, get their input. It's not that you'll necessarily put the decision to a vote. If it's your decision to make, you be the one to make it. But take the people around and under you into consideration.

Ask yourself: Is the change best for your ministry or just for you? Leaders make decisions that benefit their mission and ministry, even if the decision is costly to individuals, including themselves. If you do initiate a change, beware of wet cement. The precedent you set may well outlive you. It can harden into a policy, and you'll be stuck with it forever.

We have a deadline for camp registration at our church. We advertise, announce, and do everything but spell it out in skywriting. And every year, the day after the deadline, we get calls asking if we can squeeze one more child in . . . and then one more . . . and one more after that.

The answer is *no.*

So every year, I have disappointed adults running around saying, "That Pastor Jim is so mean! Did you know he wouldn't make an exception for me?"

That's right. The day I make an exception for one parent, I can toss the rules out the window for the rest. It will set a precedent, and I don't want to live with that for the rest of my life. Plus, all those who come after me will appreciate my not setting it.

Run the numbers.

Not all decisions have to be based on numbers, but numbers are attached to most decisions. That's reality.

Your church budget is like your house budget; some weeks are better than others for making purchases. If the youth department just bought a new sound system, you may have to wait to replace that worn-out carpet square down in the kids' classroom.

Good stewardship demands you do homework on the numbers. It may be a good decision to buy top-of-the-line cribs for the nursery because they're safest and will outlast cheaper cribs. Fine. That's a financial decision you can defend. But woe to you if you make an expensive decision you can't explain when the questions come.

Have you prayed about it?

You want to make a decision that honors God, right? So isn't it smart to ask Him if He has anything in mind? If at all possible, get the Lord's go-ahead before you make a decision. You'll sleep better!

CHAPTER 12:
ATTRACTING VOLUNTEERS

Let's say your ministry is growing. New families are coming every week, so classes and small groups are growing. There's more follow-up to do, more planning to schedule, and more people to disciple.

And when you look at your volunteers, you realize those precious folks are stretched thin. If you sardine just three more middle school boys into that classroom, their teacher will be in a hostage situation. What will you do?

Most ministry leaders immediately go into volunteer-seek mode. They ambush their friends and beg for help. They comb through the church database. They persuade the pastor to make a special announcement.

Their goal is to *get more team*, but they may have all the staff they need already but just do not know it. Or they may not be ready to handle more team, no matter how badly they could use the help. That's because when you pin them down, most ministry leaders aren't exactly sure which jobs need doing or how long those jobs will last. They aren't positive which resources they need to do the jobs that are available or how volunteers will know whether they're being successful or not.

But there's *nothing* that scares away volunteers faster than you not being clear about what you need.

Why on God's green earth would anyone sign on to follow a leader who can't describe what he or she wants? It's like showing up to help a friend move and finding that the boxes aren't ready to carry onto the truck. He's not prepared. He's wasting your time. He's not ready to direct helpers because he's still getting organized.

If you want to attract excellent volunteers, you've got to create a culture of excellence, an organization that's magnetic. Ministries like those not only attract great people, they hang onto great people.

I'm not going to list a couple dozen ways you can go out and recruit folks. I have a book that does that. What I'd like to do is back up a few steps and help you sort out the decisions you need to make *before* you start a big recruiting push.

- What sort of volunteers do you need—specifically?

- How can you recruit people who will not only help out now but help your ministry grow to the next level?

- What do you do if nobody ever seems willing to sign up? The problem may not be in your recruitment efforts—it may be in the culture of your church.

Like you, I value volunteer workers. We use over a thousand of them in our church. Without volunteers, the wheels would fall right off our ministries. But I'll tell you: I'd rather have *no* volunteers than the *wrong* volunteers. If you want to get the right people in the right spots for the right reasons, here are ten bases you'll want to cover.

1. DETERMINE EXACTLY WHAT NEEDS DOING.

Do yourself a favor: make a list of where you need help in your ministry. What jobs do you need filled? Don't just write down the bare minimum of what might work out if everything goes well and nobody calls in sick. Instead, ask yourself, "If getting excellent volunteers signed up were no problem, where and how would I use them— specifically?" Do you need a bilingual greeter? Someone to work with special-needs kids?

The fact is that you don't just need "more volunteers." You have very specific needs for specifically gifted people. Not just any warm body will do.

Who do you really need that you don't have? Create your list—now.

Next, create a flowchart of how your ministry currently looks. Write in titles and names so you can see you ministry laid out in black and white.

Look carefully at your volunteers and where they're serving. Why? Because you may discover you've got too many leaders in one place and too few in another. Instead of rounding up more bodies, you can solve your worker shortage by moving a few folks to a different area.

In my experience, ministry leaders usually think they need more people than they really need. They can't tell you where they're fully staffed, understaffed, and perfectly staffed. When we try to keep everything straight in our heads, we miss obvious in-house solutions.

And speaking of obvious, here's something for you to remember: "You have not because you ask not." Have you asked the Lord for the right people to come alongside and help you? Have you asked specific people to help? Have you asked for wisdom in planning for the future?

2. IDENTIFY THE ABILITIES YOU NEED IN VOLUNTEERS.

I think a lot of churches are like Frankenstein's monster—they have parts in the wrong places.

You remember how that big guy lurched around with knobs sticking out of his neck? Whoever built him had dropped in a heart and sewed on a head, but there were definitely parts that weren't connected quite right.

We build a little bit of a monster into our ministries when we take people and plug them into the wrong places. We forget to ask what they want to do—what they're good at—what gifts, skills, and abilities they bring with them.

Paul used the human body as an example of how spiritual gifts work. Eyes and feet don't do the same thing. If you need a foot in your ministry, then putting an eye in that spot isn't going to work out for anyone, not for the volunteer who'll feel frustrated, not for you, and not for those you are ministering to. We set people up for failure when we put them in the wrong spot.

I'm blessed in my church. The majority of our volunteers have been with us five or more of the eight years we've been a church. We've had time to sort out who's an eyeball, who's an ear, and who's a foot. And we've also been able to create positions that accommodate different commitment levels.

Not that we always get it right the first time. I once got a call from the parent of a two-year-old. She told me that every time her child came to the Wednesday night service at church number four that her child had nightmares. Being the wise person I am, I knew right away that wasn't a good thing. I also knew that if I called the teacher of that class, I'd hear that nothing was wrong. So I kept my mouth shut and visited the class the next Wednesday evening.

It was wonderful at first. There was music playing, and the children looked so happy. I thought, "That mamma doesn't know what she's talking about. There's nothing here to give a child nightmares. Her kid is off."

Then one of the teachers gathered the children around him for the lesson. He plopped a sack next to him and afterwards he said, "Tonight we're going to talk about the tongue." He reached into the sack and pulled out a three-foot cow's tongue.

The teacher wasn't an evil guy, but his kids were all teenagers. He'd forgotten what it was like to be with two-year-olds. He didn't remember that you do *not* show a three-foot tongue to two-foot people or you will inspire major nightmares. When the teacher unrolled that tongue and it flopped out at those children, there was crying and gnashing of teeth of biblical proportions in that room. And I discerned right away that I had identified the problem.

Was that teacher in the right place? No. Did he have a good heart? Yes. But he was most definitely a part out of place. So I moved him to our fourth-, fifth-, and sixth-grade classroom, and my phone started ringing off the hook. Parents called up saying, "My son can't wait to come to church. When that teacher pulls things out of his sack, boy, that's exciting." And it *was* exciting, just a bit too exciting for two-year olds.

In this case, I was able to move the volunteer to a more suitable spot, but sometimes that's not possible. Sometimes you and I will have to make the difficult decision to remove the volunteer. This checklist will help you decide.

How to Fire a Volunteer

- Do your homework. Make sure you have all the facts straight.

- Be sure you've coached the volunteer and gone the second (or even the third) mile to work with the person.

- Ask yourself, "Can the volunteer be salvaged by moving him or her to another ministry or place of service?" If so, move the person.

- Think through how this will affect your team. (Always esteem your team.)

- How will this affect your kids? (Do what's best for the kids.)

- How will this affect the volunteer in question?

- Never correct or fire a volunteer publicly. Ask for a private meeting. If you think the person is malicious or vindictive, have a witness present.

- Communicate to the volunteer that his or her actions have forced you to replace the volunteer. Do this with kindness, but be definite. Outline the actions that have prompted your decision. If you've coached the volunteer, these issues won't be a surprise.

- If the volunteer asks for another chance, give one if possible. But if the volunteer has already had multiple chances, stick by your decision.

3. DON'T ASK MORE THAN PEOPLE ARE WILLING TO GIVE.

A chicken and a pig were walking down the street when the chicken saw an old, scruffy homeless guy sitting on the sidewalk up ahead.

The homeless man looked hungry, and the chicken felt sorry for him. So the chicken nudged the pig, pointed out the homeless man, and said, "We really ought to do something. Let's give that guy some breakfast."

The pig thought it over for a moment before answering.

"That's a nice little sacrifice for you," the pig grunted, "but for me it's total commitment."

The pig understood the situation clearly. A chicken can lay an egg and walk away to tell about it. But when a pig volunteers to add bacon, ham, and sausage as side dishes, it's an entirely different story—that's *total* commitment.

When we ask people to help out in ministry, people think we're asking them to lay down their lives, to quit everything else they're doing, and to live at the church. They think we want everything on the plate, and maybe that's actually what you do want in a volunteer. If so, it's no wonder you don't have anyone around to help you.

It's great when you find lay-it-all-down pigs to join your team, but there's nothing wrong with recruiting a few chickens too. Those people are willing to faithfully do a job well but won't give every Sunday or multiple services and then show up for all the church workdays too.

There are people in my church who'll never consider teaching a class, but they'll pick up a hammer and build me anything I want. I've gone to folks and said, "I promise I'll never ask you to work in our kids' ministry if you'll give me a hundred dollars every time I ask for it." They're business people who won't miss the money. They're happy to oblige.

I phoned one guy years ago and said, "I've got seven kids who need camp scholarships. Could you write me a check for 700 dollars, please." He pulled out his checkbook without hesitation. That's not a bad deal—seven eggs with one phone call.

My point is you'll get more volunteers if you'll accept chickens as well as pigs. They'll lay eggs and be glad to do it.

4. GIVE PEOPLE JOB DESCRIPTIONS.

Put job descriptions in writing now *before* people show up. Here's why:

- You'll have a clear job description to hand a potential volunteer when God sends you that person. You and the volunteer will be talking about the same task. Your potential volunteer can make an informed decision.

- You'll avoid the temptation to create a job description based on a person rather than on the task you need done. Be sure and answer these two important questions that every volunteer has: "What do you want me to do, and how do you want me to do it?"

I once had an administrative assistant who was just outstanding. Not only was she a real bulldog when it came to protecting my time, but she was a computer-graphics whiz. In addition to helping me, she cranked out all of our publications.

When she left, I had to make a decision. Was I looking for another administrative assistant/graphic designer? Or did I need something altogether different? It had been wonderful having someone with her gifts and talents, but was that what we needed to grow to the next level?

I outlined where we were and where I saw us heading, and it became clear that what we needed was a preschool director/administrator. I could hire out the graphics stuff easily enough, but our preschool ministry was growing. I needed someone with boots on the ground who could help with it for awhile and eventually transition into that position full time.

If I had just dusted off my first administrative assistant's job description and advertised, I'd have replaced her. But I wouldn't have replaced her with someone who could do what we needed done during the next phase of our growth.

Start with describing the tasks as completely as you can, and *then* do your advertising. Bring people on board who are the right people to help you grow.

How to Write a Job Description for Volunteers

Here are a few basics:

- What will the person in this role do?

- What skills, experience, and knowledge are needed for the person to be successful?

- When do you need the job done and for how long?

- With whom will the person work? To whom will the person report?

- What will the person get out of volunteering?

Here's one example (remember, keep it short and sweet for millennials):

Do you find fulfillment in helping others?

The parking lot ministry is seeking patient, cheerful people to help visitors and church attenders move through the parking process on Sunday mornings. You'll smile at folks, pray for them as they arrive, and guide them to open parking spots.

You'll work with a team of kindhearted people and enjoy a cup of coffee and a bagel just before team rally. You'll direct traffic for that service and then be finished for the day so you can attend second service to worship.

You'll serve rain or shine, so it helps if you enjoy being out in the weather.

You'll attend monthly team nights and be expected to participate for a minimum of six months. Pastor Chrissey, our Guest Services Director, coordinates this team.

5. FOCUS ON YOUR CURRENT VOLUNTEERS.

Maybe your next superstar helper is already recruited, but you haven't taken time to coach star-level performance out of that person yet. Look for potential in people, and work with them. Don't always assume that your best helpers are still out there somewhere waiting to be lured in.

At my church, I regularly evaluate the people who report to me. That's helpful, but equally helpful is when they can evaluate themselves. People have a pretty good idea where they can use help. I ask the people who work for me to write down three areas where they want to see improvement in their skills, then together we tackle making improvements in those areas.

When we take the time to evaluate volunteers, we communicate that we expect a high level of performance. It's not enough in my children's ministry to just show up and read from the lesson materials. Kids deserve more than that. But if a volunteer does that for a few weeks yet nobody says improvement is needed, what message is sent?

I don't wait until I've got a problem to find out if people are doing what they need to do or being where they need to be. I stop by and check up weekly. I watch. I listen. Then I'm able to provide better coaching. Plus, there's another benefit—when I'm wandering around, everyone is doing their best.

Accountability helps recruit and retain volunteers because it communicates that you take what they're doing seriously—that what they're doing is important enough for you to make sure it's being done right. That matters because *nobody wants to sign up to do something that isn't important.*

6. RAISE THE SKILL LEVEL OF YOUR STAFF AND TEAM.

Here's where coaching comes in. I think ministry leaders need to be excellent coaches. We can't just be good at it; we've got to be *great*.

A good coach knows the strengths and weaknesses of his or her players, and then builds on what's there—shaping good habits and establishing strong fundamentals. They think about individual players and always ask, "What could I do to sharpen this person's skills?"

And here's what's hard for coaches: They have to let their players go out and play the game. Maybe the football coach was an all-star quarterback in his past. That doesn't matter because *coaches don't play in the games.*

I guarantee no matter how many high school football games you sit through, you'll never see a frustrated high school coach slam down his clipboard and stomp onto the field so he can throw the touchdown pass himself. Throwing the pass isn't the coach's job; teaching someone *else* to throw the pass is.

Maybe the person who takes over your favorite job won't do it exactly as you do it. That's okay. So long as the pass gets thrown and someone catches it in the end zone, the team wins.

Good coaches delight in the success of their teams rather than their own success. They catch team members doing something right, and they celebrate it. They don't need all the applause themselves—they're happy when they hear someone they train getting the ovation.

If you're coaching well, you'll hear yourself asking these questions as you watch your team members doing ministry: "What's that person doing well?" and "What can I do to help that person improve?" If you're not asking those questions, there's no way your team will get to the next level, and you'll be missing coaching opportunities.

7. RECRUIT CONSTANTLY.

Want more volunteers? So does every other ministry in your church. Your biggest competition may not be the devil or the youth group or the ushers or the parking-lot attendants. Your biggest competition may be the mindset that potential volunteers hold that they have nothing to contribute. Or your biggest competition may be how people spend their free time.

Here's a tip. Ask the church office to run a list of everybody in your church who's not volunteering anywhere. Then go find those people one at a time and personally invite them to come check out the ministry you lead.

I approach people all the time and ask, "What are you doing in this church?"

"Nothing."

"That's what I thought. Come with me."

I walk up to men in my church and say, "Listen, I need male role models for little boys and girls who don't have them in their lives. Are you willing to be an example for them?"

I've never been turned down.

There are people in your congregation who need to be needed. Find them. When you connect with those folks, they'll be the most faithful workers you've ever seen. People need to be a part of building the kingdom of God. They need to be a part of something much bigger than themselves.

The trick is to always be on the lookout for people. When you find one who might work, get their email and set up a time to get them on-boarded to the right place. Determine if the person is spiritually and emotionally suited to work on a ministry team. If it's a match, don't wait until the next recruitment drive to get that person plugged in; do it today. Now. This minute. I've never found anyone that couldn't do something for the Lord. Some people just take a minute to find what that something is.

8. USE CURRENT VOLUNTEERS TO FIND MORE VOLUNTEERS.

I don't know how to put this delicately, so I'll just say it. If you're the person in charge of finding volunteers, people in your church don't trust you. Even if they like and respect you, they're expecting you to sugarcoat things a bit when you're signing up workers. You've got a credibility problem.

But if it's your third-grade small-group leader who says that spending time with their kids each week is the highlight of her week, *she* has credibility. Why would she lie? She's not the person carrying around the sign-up sheet or trying to get them to take a picture of the QR-code sign-up form.

So ask your team to recruit more staff. Your good leaders hang out with people like them. Ask leaders to tell their buddies about your ministry. It's your job to handle screening and training, but it's not always your job to find people.

9. DETERMINE YOUR CHURCH CULTURE.

Let's say you're doing all the right things to get volunteers recruited, but nothing is happening. No new workers. Fewer returning workers. You're finding yourself pretty much in this alone. Maybe you need a serving reset.

Proverbs 22:6 KJV says, "Train up a child in the way he should go: and when he is old, he will not depart from it." That's the Bible. It's true. And one place it's true is in how people live out their Christian lives.

I was raised in a time when people believed in the old adage, "Children should be seen and not heard." That *isn't* in the Bible, by the way, but in those days it might as well have been. The adults in my life were true believers when it came to those words. We kids had our share of fun, but there were definitely times when I was supposed to sit up straight and be quiet. And the time that this sit-up-straight-and-be-quiet rule was most severely enforced was when I went to church. My job wasn't to worship or to listen or to take notes or to do anything. My job was to sit up straight and be quiet or else.

So when I got older and started going to church, what do you think I naturally did? I sat up straight and stayed quiet. That's what I'd been trained to do as a child. I had to get untrained before I could enter into worship. I had to get *untrained* before I could raise my hand to help out with doing ministry.

I guarantee you've got people in your church who were raised to sit up straight and be quiet. And you've got folks who were trained to think that the pastoral team does all the work. Those folks believe their job is to come and drop money in the offering plate or just give online. And you've got people in your church who think of youth and children's ministers as simply entertainers. They tune in once a month and watch others do ministry, but that's it.

If you want to have more volunteer workers, you've got some untraining to do. Ask yourself (and your leaders): Are people in our church trained to find places to serve? Are they trained to say *yes* to serving? Are they trained to see themselves as involved and invested?

If not, you're fighting an uphill battle when you're trying to enlist folks. Your culture doesn't support ministry. Ask for your pastor's help in changing the culture to the priesthood of the believer. What? Teach them that every believer is a minister. God has called the five-fold ministry gifts for one main purpose, "to equip his people for works of service, so that the body of Christ may be built up" (Ephesians 4:12).

10. PRAY THAT THE LORD SENDS WORKERS.

A shortage of team isn't anything new. Jesus himself described a harvest that was ready to pick, but there weren't enough workers to gather it in (Matthew 9:35-38). Your situation is probably the same. There are things you'd do if you had more team. Needs you'd meet. Families you'd reach.

If you believe more volunteers would help you accomplish what God wants accomplished through your ministry, ask God for more volunteers. Just make sure you're ready to put them to use when they show up.

Another good read that goes into more detail on this subject is my book *STRETCH: Structuring Your Ministry for Growth.*

CHAPTER 13:
STAYING MOTIVATED

I've been exercising again, and I'll tell you what, it's easier to start an exercise program than to finish it. It's also easier to do when you're younger than when you're older (which is another reason to never stop). When you're putting on running shoes and warming up, you imagine yourself out there pounding the pavement, waving to admiring people as you fly past them. But when you're actually limping along, sucking wind, hoping you remembered to carry some identification so the paramedics know who to call, that's something different.

Starting out is easy, but it's tough to finish strong, especially when you're heading uphill. So how do you stick with ministry when you hit those uphill times? When your budget is cut? When people complain? When you're taken for granted? It's at those uphill moments that it's especially hard to keep making wise personal, family, and ministry-management decisions.

Authentic leaders get discouraged just like everyone else, but they don't let themselves get stuck there. They move on.

I'd like to suggest ten ways you can move past discouragement.

1. DO WHAT YOU DO FOR THE RIGHT REASONS.

Colossians 3:23 tells us to do whatever we do with all of our heart for the Lord. That means you're not just working for a paycheck. You're not even just working for your leaders. You're working for the Lord.

I've already outlined some reasons leaders fail, but your goal isn't just to avoid failure —it's to be a success! And success in ministry is measured ultimately by hearing, "Well done, good and faithful servant."

Are you making decisions to please God or people?

Are you leading people the direction God wants to take them? Are you in it for the right reasons?

If your motivations are anything other than pure, seek wise counsel and confess your shortcomings. Remember, excellent, motivated, and lasting leadership springs from a heart that's right with Father.

2. REALIZE IT'S YOUR JOB TO STAY MOTIVATED.

It's not your leader's job to keep you motivated and growing. It's not your church's job. It's your job.

When I read the story of Moses, I see that Aaron and Hur encouraged and supported Moses. But ultimately, it was Moses who had to decide to keep his arms in the air.

Let me be clear. *It's not your leader's job to keep you fired up.* I serve pastors who are never too busy for me to contact them and ask them to spend time with me, and it's a blessing. But whether or not my leader provides motivation and coaching, I still need to do what's on my to-do list to the best of my ability.

Take responsibility for staying enthusiastic about your ministry. Don't count on others to do that for you or to be your cheerleaders.

3. STAY IN THE WORD OF GOD.

Whenever you're shaken, what you've filled your life with is what will come out.

When problems arise in your ministry and shake you, if you're full of pride, then pride will pour out of you. If you're full of anger, that's what will spill out and splash on others. But if you've been in the Word of God, faithful in spiritual disciplines, then that's what comes out.

Quiet time is one way to stay in God's Word, but let me add another one that lots of people in ministry seem to overlook: Go to church. Don't go to lead but to get on your knees and worship God with your whole heart. Soak up God's love surrounded by other people doing the same thing.

I understand that if you're in the ministry, Sunday is a workday for you. And if you're in a church with one service, I'm sorry because that puts you at a real disadvantage. But you still need to find a way to go to church frequently, no matter what. There is nothing like being in the presence of Almighty God!

Go for your own spiritual nourishment. Go to support your leadership. Go so people see you and know if they sign up to help with the ministry program that you're over, they can still go to church too. Ask a strong leader you've discipled and poured your heart into to stand in your place and watch over the program while you worship. We call that a 2IC at my church. (That stands for "2nd In Charge," and you should be developing lots of them!) If they need you, they can text you.

4. PRAY CONTINUALLY.

Things happen when you pray. In your situation. In your life. In other peoples' lives. And I believe those things *only* happen when you pray.

Pray, and you'll have a more powerful, effective ministry. And when you see how God acts in and through you, that's tremendous motivation. I read this on a church sign once. It may be cheesy, but I've never forgotten it: "If you hem your ministry and life with prayer, it's less likely to unravel."

5. CHOOSE TO STAY HAPPY.

I'll tell you what, life is just too short to not have fun.

I don't know your situation or the challenges you're facing at church, home, or with your health; but Paul didn't know your situation either, yet he had some great advice for you and me both: "Rejoice always, pray continually, give thanks in all circumstances; for this is God's will for you in Christ Jesus" (1 Thessalonians 5:17,18).

I've yet to meet a thankful person who wasn't also happy.

Find people who make you laugh, and hang around them. Cultivate those people, and invest in them.

I make at least two pilgrimages a year to guitar shows—one in Dallas and one in Arlington. And I've made it a point to pull together a group of guitar-playing buddies who come with me. If you met these guys, you'd wonder how we could ever get along. There's a dentist who's really conservative and another guy who's a true good-ole-boy redneck. Then there's the old hippie hairdresser. And there's another guy who has played in bands all his life but now owns his own chair company—he's a great player and a great guy. Then there's me—the old children's pastor. What a crew!

I love those trips, and I enjoy those guys enormously. The dentist eggs on the redneck, we play jokes on each other, and we laugh until we cry. Being with those guys makes me happy. We've been doing this now for so long that we have to go back to the hotel and take a nap before dinner, so we can stay up!

Who makes you happy? Why aren't you seeing those people more?

6. KEEP DOING WHAT GOD'S CALLED YOU TO DO.

Once you're in leadership, it's easy to get pulled into doing things that aren't really part of your calling. And when you quit doing what you're supposed to be doing, ministry can get discouraging fast.

In 1983, God spoke to me and told me to quit doing kids' crusades. I'd done dozens of them. I liked doing them. I was pretty good at it too. God told me to quit "handing out fish sandwiches"; instead, I was to teach people to fish. Father told me He was going to open doors for me to teach teachers and train people to be better leaders.

My function since that day has been to teach teachers and coach others to train people how to fish! I've been doing it in addition to building children's programs in great churches for 46 years and counting, but it's never been a question in my mind if I should stop helping other leaders. God hasn't told me to quit doing it yet, so here I am, leading conferences, providing training resources, and writing books. When a lot of my friends are retiring, I'm refocusing and hanging out with younger people year after year. It's motivating and fulfilling to do what God wants.

Where's your place in the Body of Christ? What's your function? Are you there yet? If so, don't get weary in well doing!

7. LEAD PEOPLE WHO WILL FOLLOW.

The most discouraging, demotivating thing that ever happened to me in ministry has to be the time I called a worker meeting and three people showed up—me, my wife, and my mother-in-law. That was a low point. I was just getting started at my first church. The church had just hired me as their first-ever Christian Education Director. And when I got on board, all the volunteers figured they could quit.

But I had a little group of sixth-graders who thought helping out was a big deal, so I worked with them, and we formed a puppet team. I'd have rather had a bunch of adult helpers, but none were willing. So I led the people willing to follow—a little group of sixth-graders. (Now those kids are in their mid-fifties!) Pretty soon they got their parents involved, and then the program took off. But if I had sat around sulking, nothing would have happened.

You probably don't have all the volunteers or servant leaders you'd like to have. There are people you want who won't sign up. Forget about them. Lead people who will follow. (Also be sure and read my book *Building Teams That Stick: Creating a Serving Reset*.)

8. MENTOR SOMEONE ELSE.

When you mentor someone else, you set an example for them. Someone wise is depending on you to stay motivated so they can learn. I don't know about you, but I rise to that sort of challenge.

Who are you mentoring? What sort of example are you setting?

9. BE A SELF-STARTER.

You know what your function in the Body of Christ is, right? Let's say your role is to equip small-group leaders to be effective in their small groups. Then why not reach out to people in other churches with the same calling, and ask them what they can teach you? Search the Web to see what Google can tell you. Reach out to that speaker that taught that workshop or webinar you attended last year, and set up a Zoom call.

Become a student of your job. Search for ways to get more information, better skills, and a broader perspective. Always keep learning. There's a lot of motivation that comes with growing in your abilities and advancing your program.

Also, get *evaluated*. If there's no evaluation procedure at your church, create one. Ask people above you to describe your strengths and weaknesses, and ask the workers who serve beneath you to do the same thing. These are people who see you in action. What are they seeing? Invite them to tell you.

10. REFUSE TO QUIT.

Until I came to church number four, there was a pattern in my life: Every three-to-four years, I'd switch churches. I'd hit year three in a ministry setting, and that's where I sort of would lose momentum, so I left. I was giving up too soon.

I've watched ministry leaders, and I've observed that they really don't master their situations until the *fifth* year . . . at least I haven't.

Here's the truth. Leaders who give up and move on seldom find greener grass at another church. They hit the same walls there, too, and usually the same year as their former church.

Decide to stick where you are. Ask God for grace to grow in your leadership. One thing is for sure—it won't be boring.

CHAPTER 14:
HOW TO BECOME A NEXT-LEVEL LEADER

A few years ago, I was selected by *Children's Ministry* magazine as one of ten "Pioneers of the Decade" in children's ministry. There was my picture smiling out at the readers of the magazine. It was an honor, but it also got me thinking. *What was next for me? How could I take my ministry to the next level of service, effectiveness, and faithfulness? Would it ever be time to just coast?*

For each of us, there's a next level of leadership. Whether we're just surviving or we're thriving and setting the world on fire, there's a next level for us. It's the level where we go from being *good* to being excellent.

What we did at church number four was pretty good. *Very* good. But there was always room for us to get better, to redefine the word excellent. As a leader, there's always room for me to sharpen my skills. I did that at church number 5 and am pursuing my next level today at church number 6.

I've talked with dozens of excellent leaders. They're people whose ministries are growing, sometimes against all odds. They're influencing their communities. And they have a passion for their ministry and the people they're serving that is simply unstoppable.

I believe there are sixteen marks of a next-level leader who's growing rather than just maintaining. Most of these people aren't any smarter than you and me. They don't always have bigger budgets. They don't have superpowers. What nudges these leaders from good to *excellent* has less to do with what they've got than with who they are. We'd do well to ask God to give us these sixteen characteristics in even greater measure.

I've touched on a few of these characteristics already, but let's look at them all together now, and we'll see what next-level leaders look like.

1. NEXT-LEVEL LEADERS ARE DRIVEN PEOPLE.

The idea of being "driven" has gotten a bad reputation. We think of driven people as living out-of-balance lives. We think they're out for glory and recognition. That's not at all what I mean.

Driven leaders are motivated by a desire to excel in the work God has placed before them. They'll do whatever it takes to go from "good enough" to "excellent."

They'll study harder. Pray longer. Stretch themselves further. Work smarter. Master something they've never been able to do. They'll plug away until they have the skills to effectively lead others in ministry. They'll have enthusiasm for what they're doing.

Driven leaders may not work more hours than we do, but they're always thinking, always making connections that will improve their ministries. They're not motivated solely by a paycheck.

Here are questions only you can answer: *Are you doing ministry but also watching the clock?* Do you save your most productive, most creative hours for hobbies instead of your ministry? Are you giving your best?

2. NEXT-LEVEL LEADERS KNOW WHERE THEY ARE.

If you want to travel somewhere, you've got to have a destination. But before you get started, you need to know where you are. Otherwise, you don't know what direction will take you closer to your destination.

I knew a guy who went on a youth group ski trip to Colorado. The group members started out in Tulsa, and about the time they hit Kansas, somebody pulled out a map to see how far they still had to go. Well, it was a lot farther than they expected because they were headed *east*, but Colorado is *west*.

They discovered that their enthusiasm to reach Colorado didn't much matter because they were headed the wrong direction. They had their destination in mind, but they hadn't nailed down their starting point on the map.

Next-level leaders assess where they are. They have a realistic, no-nonsense understanding of precisely where they're sitting. And they have a step-by-step plan to get where they're headed.

Can you give a concise description of where you are in your ministry? What do the next steps look like? How do you intend to get to your destination?

3. NEXT-LEVEL LEADERS KNOW WHERE THEY'RE GOING.

Excellent leaders can actually *see* their vision. They can *taste* it. They *hear* the sounds of children playing on a playground that hasn't yet been built. They *smell* the new seats of church buses that their checkbook says they can't possibly afford. They're determined to go where they believe God calls them, and the journey energizes them.

If a next-level leader believes God has called her to double the number of kids in Sunday school, she plans with that number in mind. She talks about that number at meetings and writes it on whiteboards. Her enthusiasm becomes contagious, and pretty soon she's surrounded by people who share her vision.

Listen to yourself at your next staff meeting. Do you sound as if you know where you're going? Do you hear yourself talking about little goals or big ones? Do you have a vision that gets people excited?

4. NEXT-LEVEL LEADERS HAVE THEIR PERSONAL LIVES IN ORDER.

Ready for a test? Ask your family if they feel more important than your job. Ask your spouse. Ask your friends.

What did they say? Next-level leaders lead a balanced life that makes room for family and friends. Excellent leaders know that life is a marathon, not a sprint. Committees come and go; family is forever.

5. NEXT-LEVEL LEADERS KEEP CHANGING THEIR DEFINITION OF EXCELLENCE.

When they achieve a goal, next-level leaders don't stop and build a monument to their success. They reassess, set new goals, and move toward a new goal, a new definition of success.

A while back, I got in the mail a baseball card signed by a fellow who plays for the Marlins. He reminded me of the times we played together back in children's church when he was a little guy. He sent the card to let me know he'd reached his dream; he was playing in the big leagues.

Thousands of kids play little league, but very few make the little league all-star team. Of those young all-stars, few go on to play in high school. Fewer high school players play on a college team, and it's a very rare college player who's asked to play in the minor leagues. And of the hundreds of players competing on minor- league teams, few make it to the majors.

I guarantee that a little leaguer's definition of baseball excellence is different from a high schooler's definition. What cuts it in college isn't good enough for the pros. For each level of play you want to move up, your definition needs to change.

6. NEXT-LEVEL LEADERS PLAN AHEAD . . . WAY AHEAD.

The best time to plan for next year's VBS is the day after this year's VBS ends. That's when your team is already assembled. That's when everyone remembers all the details, when you've got all the receipts and attendance charts in front of you. If you wait eight months to sit down and plan, you'll be lost.

Next-level leaders keep calendars that stretch out two or more years ahead. Not everything happens as they predict, but they still plan ahead. Excellence requires it.

How far ahead do you plan? What would change for you and your ministry if you doubled that time-frame?

7. NEXT-LEVEL LEADERS DELEGATE.

A next-level leader can look at a to-do list and know what's most important to do. And that excellent leader will know what *not* to do.

Forget that old idea that excellent leaders know exactly what's happening everywhere in their organization. Really excellent leaders don't have a clue as to some of the details, but they know who does know. They've delegated some of their tasks and responsibilities to trustworthy people.

Look, if the devil wants to keep you from being successful in your ministry, he probably won't be able to trick you into taking drugs. And it's unlikely you'll suddenly leave your spouse to start embezzling the kids' mission offerings. But if you can be persuaded to spend all your time doing the wrong things, you'll be just as ineffective as if you were off doing some horrible sin. Next-level leaders don't do everything. They do only the things they can do, and they have other people do the rest.

Wait a minute. I hear you sayin, "Pastor Jim, that's great for you. You've got tons of staff and volunteers to share the load. But I'm sitting here with a staff of just three— me, myself, and I. If I don't do things myself, they just won't get done."

Then don't do it. If you honestly can't take on another project, say so. Let that task sit until you raise up someone alongside you to help. If you pull all-nighters and ignore your health and your family to get it done, then you'll never get any help. Why? Because you've proven you can do it yourself.

8. NEXT-LEVEL LEADERS BRING ORDER.

Next-level leaders bring order to a ministry by thinking through the steps it takes to reach goals, even goals that may be years away. Here's how I learned that lesson.

I wanted a worship band for our junior-high ministry, but I couldn't find a drummer. Then I happened to look at the stage where the band would play, and I realized we didn't have any drums. Even if God had miraculously raised up a dozen drummers, I couldn't have used them. No drums. So we got a set of drums up there, and a drummer soon followed.

I was trying to go from *no band* straight to *complete band*. I hadn't thought through the steps that would get us there. Next-level leaders often do that sort of thinking on flowcharts. They can tell you the steps from point A to point Z.

Don't wait until you're a huge church to establish a culture of order. At number four, we didn't. If you're a small church, act now to do the things that you'll be forced to do when you're a large church.

There was a time at church number 4 we had two buses. If you wanted a bus for your ministry activity, you'd have to walk through the church office shouting, "Anybody using the bus next Friday?" If nobody hollered back, you assumed you'd reserved a bus. I can't tell you how many times we got to the church and found the youth group, kid's ministry, and senior citizens all standing in the parking lot, all expecting to use the same bus.

So I asked myself, "If we had one hundred buses, how would we operate?" I came up with a bus policy, and ten years later, we had sixty-five buses. We imposed order on a chaotic situation, and it made everyone's life easier. When I left that church, we had 100 vehicles and were using that same system.

What are the organizational things that bug you? That keep happening again and again? Those are probably items you can change for the better by creating policies and procedures to address them.

9. NEXT-LEVEL LEADERS TRAIN THEIR PEOPLE.

Let me be clear what I mean by training. I want to be specific because Christians tend to confuse talking with training.

At many churches, new volunteers are trained with a short lecture and then handed a job, thrown to work, and told not to quit until Jesus returns. But true training is placing your new recruit alongside someone who knows what she's doing and letting your recruit watch awhile. You're new recruit gets hands-on experience and coaching, plus the chance to ask questions.

When the new recruit knows he can handle it, you give him some responsibility. Then, after he proves himself, you give him a bit more. And when he's mastered that, he gets even more. And on it goes.

Write this down in the margin: *There is no shortcut to training.* It takes what it takes. Excellent leaders understand that and invest in their people accordingly.

10. NEXT-LEVEL LEADERS CONNECT WITH OTHER LEADERS.

Some leaders become uncomfortable around strong leaders. I've seen very capable children's ministry leaders get tongue-tied and nervous around their senior pastor. And for the life of me, I can't figure out why.

Listen, other than your mother, there's nobody in the world who wants to see you succeed in your ministry to kids more than your senior pastor. One secret to your pastor's success is what you're doing over in the children's department. Your pastor is on your side, so why would you be nervous when your pastor strolls through the children's area to see what's up?

Mark my words: If you're uncomfortable dealing with strong leaders, you'll never be one yourself. *Don't let someone's title or paycheck intimidate you; you're serving someone who owns the sheep on a thousand hills.* If you're doing good work, you have no reason to feel inferior to anyone.

11. NEXT-LEVEL LEADERS FOCUS ON MEETING NEEDS.

There's a difference between a program and a ministry. Don't create a program without first being able to describe what need it's designed to meet.

A while back, the church I was serving decided to do something special for the college kids. All of us pastor-types sat down to discuss what we should do, and eventually a radical idea popped up: Why didn't we just ask them? We had our ideas, but maybe they'd have some insight to offer too. So we called in some college kids and asked them what kind of program would be meaningful to them and why. Our ideas weren't even close.

Now we base every program on meeting a need in the lives of our children, youth, adults, or families. And we don't guess—we ask. We ask kids, parents, and other leaders.

What are the needs of people in your church and community? How do your programs address those needs? When was the last time you evaluated those needs? Next-level leaders meet the needs of the people they serve.

12. NEXT-LEVEL LEADERS MANAGE PEOPLE WELL.

If you're in ministry, you're in the people business. And to have a successful ministry, you absolutely must build and coach a strong team. The place to begin managing people is to love them and want what's best for them. That attitude and commitment will help you now and when it's time to give your team suggestions and correction.

The fact is that if you don't care about me and you don't want what's best for me, why *should* I care what you think? You just want to be large and in charge. That's a far cry from being a beloved leader.

Let me just ask you this: Do you love your volunteers? (Do you like them?) If you love them, how do they know? How are you communicating your love?

13. NEXT-LEVEL LEADERS ARE PROBLEM SOLVERS.

It's one thing to see the shortcomings in your ministry. It's another thing to fix them.

Here's something we did at church number four. We worked to eliminate excuses. When we planned a ministry program, we asked *upfront* what the excuses would be for not participating. Then we work to eliminate the reasons for those excuses before launching the program.

At one time, we found it hard to recruit bus captains—they were the people in charge of our bus routes. So we asked, "What excuses will we hear when we ask someone to serve in our bus ministry?" The answer was obvious. Bus-ministry captains had to give up every Saturday, all year long, to call on kids on their routes. Would you do that? *I* sure wouldn't.

So I told my pastor I wanted to shorten the hours bus-ministry folks did visits, so on holidays and four-day weekends when most kids weren't home anyway, we didn't go out. That took us from asking a volunteer for 52 Saturdays per year down to 36 Saturdays. We eliminated an unrealistic expectation.

What excuses do you hear when people don't want to serve in your children's ministry? What can you do, without compromising the quality and effectiveness of your program, to eliminate those excuses *before* you ask for volunteers?

Check out Chapter 10 on becoming an effective problem solver for help with sharpening this skill.

14. NEXT-LEVEL LEADERS LEARN FROM OTHER LEADERS.

Proverbs 27:17 says, "As iron sharpens iron, so one person sharpens another." Your leadership won't grow from *good* to *excellent* if you sit alone in your study. You've got to go rub shoulders with people who are doing things right. Visit other churches, and don't look at their shortcomings; look for their strengths.

Call up business leaders in your community, and ask them what they're doing to motivate their people, to read the culture, and to grow in their influence and market share. See what you can apply to your situation. And if the vice president of marketing at Widget International gets intrigued with what you're up to, share the Gospel with him so he understands.

Don't just stand on the sidelines watching other leaders. Ask them why they made the decisions they did and what they saw or heard in situations that you missed. Squeeze every bit of coaching possible from time spent with excellent leaders.

And you don't even have to meet with every leader face to face who you admire. Just look at what you're reading. I studied Colin Powell's book because if he could run the US military, I figured he could help me organize our nursery. If Lee Iacocca could straighten out Chrysler, I thought he might have a few ideas for my preschool. I read Sam Walton's book because the guy who built the biggest retail organization in America might offer some suggestions that would help my elementary program grow. And I pondered the leadership principles of Abraham Lincoln because if he could put a war-torn country back together, he must have something to say that will help my youth group.

What's on your reading list this month? Anything that will stretch your leadership? What other leaders are you meeting and interviewing? Remember, you can tell a lot about a leader by the company he or she keeps.

15. NEXT-LEVEL LEADERS DON'T TRY TO DO IT ALONE.

Don't believe for a minute you can build a super-ministry all by yourself. It won't happen.

Winning coaches know that winning takes more than a strong first string. It takes a strong bench too. If the same people always lead worship or preach in children's church, what happens when those people move on? You've got to be developing your next team, letting those second stringers get some playing time.

And what happens if you move on? If God calls you to another church or calls you home, what happens to the ministry you've built?

There is no success without a successor. If you love the kids and volunteer workers in your care, you'll have a plan in place to fill your shoes.

16. NEXT-LEVEL LEADERS HAVE A SHEPHERD'S HEART.

Some people are in leadership for all the wrong reasons. They enjoy power and privileges. They like calling the shots. They feel bigger when they order others around. But leadership in the church isn't about getting power. It's never been about getting power. In the kingdom of God, it's those willing to serve who please God.

If you're in ministry, you'd better be there because you've got a shepherd's heart. You'll be successful only when you're determined to serve God and the people He's placed around you. *Next-level leaders are next-level servants.*

How do people describe you? Are you a leader who's there to serve or to be served?

It's been my experience that next-level leaders—leaders who move from *good* to *excellent*—are characterized by the traits we've just discussed. I think these traits are so important that I've included a list of them on the next page. Post it where you'll see it often. Pray through it regularly.

THE NEXT-LEVEL LEADER'S PRAYER

Lord, when I'm serving You and Your people, "good enough" just isn't good enough. I want to lead and serve with excellence.

Today, give me opportunities to grow in You. I want to become a leader who

- is driven and dedicated.

- knows where I'm going.

- knows where I am.

- has my personal life in order.

- keeps changing my definition of excellence.

- plans ahead . . . way ahead.

- delegates.

- brings order.

- trains my people.

- connects with other leaders. • focuses on meeting needs.

- manages people well.

- is a problem solver.

- learns from other leaders.

- has a shepherd's heart.

Lord, thanks for the privilege of serving. In Jesus' name, amen.

CHAPTER 15:
LESSONS FROM A FORGIVEN FATHER

I asked someone in children's ministry the other day if she was full time at her church. What a silly question!

Of course, she's full time at her church. They may pay her for full time, part time, or not give her a nickel, but she's still working full time. I don't know anyone in children's ministry who's *not* full time. It's just that sort of job.

I've already mentioned that when I started in children's ministry, I left a secular job and gave up my spot in a band for less money than I was making in the band. I didn't just take a pay *cut*, I took a pay *amputation*. But because my wife and I knew it was the Lord's will, I went full time at the church. I was so excited that I'd be able to work full time with boys and girls. What a tremendous opportunity!

I soon discovered that I'd had more time for kid contact when I was a volunteer. As a staff person, I now had days designated for counseling and hospitals visitations. The shut-in ministry and a ton of administrative stuff landed on my plate too. If I wanted to take care of all that and have kid contact, I'd be working more than forty or fifty hours a week, that's for sure. And you're probably in the same boat. Ministry always takes more time than you expect, and *excellent* ministry under the guidance of Holy Spirit also takes more time than you expect.

Here's the tension. How can you be an excellent Spirit-led ministry leader and an excellent spouse and an excellent parent at the same time? When we look at our ministry to-do list, it sometime feels as if we're expected to sacrifice our families on the altar of ministry, doesn't it?

Well, don't you do it. You can't afford to do it. There's another way.

MINISTRY STARTS AT HOME

I believe that from the get-go, we've got to first and foremost minister to and care for our families. This isn't just my opinion either. I believe it's what God's Word teaches. After all, God established the home *before* He established the church. And 1 Timothy 3:5 says, "If anyone does not know how to manage his own family, how can he take care of God's church?"

I know a lot of people in ministry who have this backward. They take care of the church first and then they worry about home. They think their church work is more important than their home. Not true.

If you're a parent, your primary ministry is with your own family. I always tell children's pastors, if they win every kid in their city for Jesus, but they don't have time for their own children, I believe they're a failure. If that seems harsh, I'm sorry, but I think it's true. You've got a God-given responsibility to tend first to your own children and then to other kids. I am married to my family, and I date the church. It's not the other way around.

Read Deuteronomy 6:6-7; it's the parents' responsibility to train up their children in the things of the Lord. It's not something that can be delegated to a children's pastor. And if you are the children's pastor, it's not something you can hand off to your spouse or to the children's program at your church.

Listen, we all know horror stories about ministry leaders whose kids can't stand going to church and who reject the things of God. One reason is that often these kids learned early on that for Daddy or Mommy, church was more important. I have friends in ministry whose children aren't living for God. These are children old enough to be making their own lifestyle decisions, and, unfortunately, they're choosing to not honor God.

My friends would give anything—anything—to turn their children around, but they can't. It's up to their kids now to make their own decisions. These parents did what they could. They're still doing what they can, but I'm sure there's not a day that goes by without their wondering if there's something else they could have done. That's not a discussion you want to be having with yourself in a few years, so focus on your children now. Teach them. Disciple them. Encourage them. Have fun with them!

And give them a home where they know that they're more important than your career, not just by your words but also by your deeds. The other day my pastor answered a phone call from her daughter on the stage during a church service. It was one of the best examples of the priority of a godly mom I had ever witnessed. You see, it was right after we had major flooding in our city and there were road closures all around us. My pastor knew her teenage daughter needed help navigating a safe passage for her and her brother. She demonstrated firsthand that she was a mom first and a pastor second. It was powerful and truly an amazing teaching moment for our church.

I can't fill the role of daddy for every child in Nashville. God has called me to be the father of two wonderful girls, father-in-law of their husbands, and the grandfather of my incredible grandkids. That's it. I can be an example to other kids, and I want to, but they can find other examples. I can be a leader in the lives of other kids, but I want to help reach and empower parents to be the moms and dads God wants them to be, so I must model this for them to see firsthand.

My two girls can never find another Daddy. That's where I can't be replaced, and I don't want to be replaced; so I choose to guard this precious opportunity.

If you don't have kids, don't think you're off the hook. Are you married? Then your first priority needs to be your home, not the children's or youth or small-group ministries.

It's my wish that Julie never regrets for a day that she married me. That she knows every day that I love her, cherish her, and thank God for her. I want my marriage to be strong and fulfilling for both of us.

Spending all my time at the church or every night of the week at a meeting or always glued to a computer screen won't get me what I want or give Julie what she deserves. It won't create a home that honors Father or that is a great place to live. God established my home. I'm not being a poor leader if I protect and dedicate it for His glory and for His purposes.

MOSES MESSED UP . . . BIG TIME

Figuring out how to balance being a ministry leader and a family leader isn't a new problem. Neither is failing to do it correctly.

In Exodus 18:2-6, we see that Moses is having some trouble at home—big trouble! He and his family have separated, and Moses has sent away his wife Zipporah and their two sons. The three go to live with Moses' father-in-law, Jethro. But Jethro is a smart guy. He doesn't let them stay long. He brings them back to Moses, and then he sticks around for a few days to see if he can figure out the problem.

Jethro discovers Moses is wearing himself out in ministry. Moses is wearing out the people of Israel too. And if Jethro was the father I think he was, when he had a heart-to-heart talk with Moses, I'm sure he also threw in, "And this isn't real good for my daughter and grandkids either."

Now there is nothing wrong with Moses wanting to do a good job as a leader. But Moses had crossed a critical line. He'd sacrificed his family for his ministry.

Listen, *you cannot build your ministry on the ashes of your family*. You can't say, "I'm doing this for God, so He'll just have to take care of my spouse and kids." Your family must be your first priority, not in the future after you've made it through the Easter play, or after you've got your second service up and running, or after you get a bigger church. Your family has to come first now. You won't be able to take your spouse on a vacation next year and somehow make up for treating them as a second-class project this year.

I'll be honest, when I first started in ministry, I had a hard time balancing ministry and family life. Like Moses, I wasn't organized enough at church to keep my job under control. That put me in a hole both at work *and* at home. I've straightened that out, asked forgiveness, and it has been absolutely worth the effort.

If you want to be an effective leader, find a way to put your family first. Letting your family take a back seat to your ministry is a surefire way to not only ruin your home life but undermine your effectiveness as a leader.

Maybe you've got this all under control. Fine. Now test it. Ask everyone in your family: Have you ever felt that you were less important than my church work? If so, when? And how did that make you feel?

Ask your kids and your spouse to be honest and mean it.

And even if you hear that you're always available, always attentive, and always wonderful, find ways to improve.

I believe that it's never too late to fall in love with your family and for them to fall in love with you. You may have high school kids who've checked out of family life, but if they're still in your house, you can start doing things right. You can reach out to them. You can confess that you have had your priorities out of alignment, and then you can make changes that will influence them and their behavior.

Here are ten keys to building a strong family in a ministry household. I know they work because they've worked for me.

1. HAVE A VISION FOR YOUR FAMILY.

We set visions for our ministries, so why not our families?

What's your vision for how your family will look and behave? For how you'll serve God together? For how each member of your family will develop his or her individual gifts for serving? What do your children want to accomplish?

If you don't set goals for your family, you're aiming at nothing in particular, and I can guarantee you'll hit it. Everyone will get older, maybe your kids will get married and have kids, and sooner or later everyone will die. Is that all you're after?

My two children are as different as night and day. They don't even look like sisters. The younger one is six inches taller than the older one. They have different colors of hair, different temperaments, and completely different goals.

God made my daughters unique people, and he put them in our family for a reason. I want to help them both develop their gifts and find a way to use those gifts to serve God. That's not the job of their church leaders or even their small-group leaders— that's the job of their parents.

What's the vision for your family? For each member of your family?

2. DESIRE TO BE CLOSE.

Psalm 37:4 says, "Take delight in the Lord, and he will give you the desires of your heart." I had a retired next-door neighbor in Tulsa that was a handy guy to live next door to. After he had fixed up everything at his house, he started hanging around my house and fixing things. I'd come home, and the gate would have been re-hung. He'd call us and say that since he's picking up fertilizer for his yard, he'll pick it up for our yard too. This was not a bad deal.

In the process, he'd gotten a close-up look at our family because we had a *lot* of things that needed fixing. One day he said something to Julie that just broke our hearts: "Your family is so close. Watching your family makes me wish I had wanted a close family when my kids were little."

His granddaughter came to visit occasionally, but he hardly ever saw his son. My neighbor shook his head and said, "I really made some mistakes. I just didn't desire a close family. There were other things I wanted instead."

Don't get me wrong. I don't think my neighbor was a bad man. He was trying to provide for his kids during the years they were under his roof. But that didn't communicate love to his kids, and he didn't have a desire to connect. That's a decision that cost him.

Believe me, if you're going to have a family that survives the ministry, you'll need a family that desires to be close. And I believe with all my heart that part of what will earn you a "well done, my good and faithful servant," will be how you lead at home, not just at church.

3. SCHEDULE TIME TO BE WITH YOUR FAMILY.

Is your family important enough to you to rate a spot in your schedule? Mine is, and they know it. They can open my calendar and see their names right there in bold print.

One thing my wife and I like doing is walking together each day. Besides my needing the exercise and to get my steps in (thanks, Apple Watch), there's the added bonus of entertaining the neighbors as they see my cute, thin wife walking her big ole' husband around the neighborhood. I think they get a chuckle out of that.

And for us, there's the bonus of having time together. We get to talk—*without distractions*—and that's a treat. Whenever a few days have gone by and our schedules have kept us from walking, Julie will say, "I really miss our walks." That's my cue. I know I need to go walking, not just for the exercise but because she needs time with me. And you know what? I need that time too.

Communicate your schedule to your spouse. My wife has been in ministry with me for more than forty years, so she and I both know when the busy times will be. She knows when I'm going to miss a week or two of dinners because I'm at church preparing for a big event. But I still check in with her to make sure she knows she's important. I still call if I'll miss a dinner. And I expect her to do the same with me.

I'm a big believer in us doing things together. My wife once said that she thought we needed a hobby we could do together. I figured she'd suggest golf or something like that. But she said, "I'd like to start shooting."

"Shooting?"

"With a pistol," she said.

So for Mother's Day, I got my little wife a pistol. Being a good redneck, I already had four or five, so I knew right where to go to get her one. And then, every so often, we'd go out shooting. Sometimes we'd take the girls. We called those outings "lead fests." There the Wideman family would be, out in the middle of nowhere, shooting up a storm. I'm not suggesting that target shooting is necessarily the activity you should do together as a couple or as a family, but find something that you enjoy together, and do it.

I'll tell you this though. Before my daughters found their husbands, I wanted every boy who even thought of dating one of them to take note that their daddy and mommy had pistols, and we knew how to use them. For that matter, I wanted them to know that my *daughters* were pretty good shots too.

4. GO ON DATES.

When you schedule time to be with your family, you're honoring and serving your family. And when you schedule dates with your wife or husband, you're just being smart.

If I intend to keep my wife's affection, I have to keep doing what I did to win her heart in the first place. I've got to keep calling her and going to fun places with her. I give her cards and flowers. I spend money on her. When I go out with her, I clean up as best I can because I want to show her that I'm honored to be with her. It's a matter of respect. That's what I did when we were dating, so why would I stop now?

And may I suggest another way to spend time with your family? Tag along when someone is running errands. At our house, Julie does most of the grocery shopping. I don't particularly care to go shopping, but it's an awfully cheap date, especially if I don't put extra stuff in the cart.

I used to hate shopping centers, but my daughters loved to shop. And when I'd go with them, we had a great time. My grands love to go with me to Target because they know G and GG are going to bless them. Here's my point. When you venture into your family members' worlds, you communicate that you care. With a little effort, you can redeem "chore time" and turn it into "communication time." Almost anytime together can be special if you approach it with the right attitude.

One final piece of advice, don't forget getaways! Agree on the frequency that you and your spouse will get away alone for a long weekend, even if you're busy, well, *especially* if you're busy. The church members will understand and so will your pastors.

5. DISCIPLE YOUR CHILDREN.

Matthew 28:19 is pretty clear: "Therefore, go and make disciples of all nations, baptizing them in the name of the Father and of the Son and of the Holy Spirit." Somewhere in one of those nations are your children. It's your job to disciple them, and that, my friend, takes time.

If you want to see your children grow in the Lord, you've got to make a commitment to be together as a family and also to regularly spend time with each of your children. Just last night, I took my youngest daughter, Whitney, and her husband out for sushi. The rest of my family won't touch the stuff, especially my grands, so this is something that we can do together that is special. (Whitney was also my ride-rides-at-Disney buddy.)

My other daughter, Yancy, and I love to catch concerts together. We like to take binoculars to concerts and try to figure out what kind of gear the musicians are using. People who sit next to us think we're nuts, but we don't care. We have a good time.

No way could I switch activities with my girls. They have unique likes and dislikes, and I know that because I've entered into their worlds. When they lived at home, I knew what brand of clothing they each liked. I also knew that now and then, because they like to dress up, I was going to get dragged off to the Dove Awards or a musical or a ballet.

If you want to disciple your children, you've got to consistently be in their lives looking for teachable moments and watching for chances to share God's Word. That's also true with grands. You can't pass faith down if you're not spending time with them.

Confession—I've never been much of a family-devotion guy. I'm not big on setting aside half an hour every week to get religious with my family. I think our *entire life together* needs to be a devotion! I talk about the Word and how it fits into our daily life as daily life unfolds. Are devotions good? Sure, but so is being always on the alert for opportunities to discuss life as it happens. I follow Holy Spirit's lead to point out Jesus everywhere I can.

I'm big on praying with my kids and grands, and I hope you are too. Raising a child requires prayer, so you might as well include that child in the process.

Are you spending time with each member of your family? Do you know your spouse's favorite flower and movie? Each child's favorite activity and music genre? You earn the right to disciple your family when they believe you love them. Give your family members all the evidence in the world that you're crazy about each of them.

6. TRAIN YOUR CHILDREN.

Your kids need your example. It's one thing to *tell* them what's right and another thing to *show* them. That's when lessons get memorable.

Make a list of all the things you want your children and grands to be, of all the character traits and all the personality traits you want them to exhibit when they grow up. Identify the fruits of the Spirit you want them to model. Then get busy becoming those things yourself so you can be a model.

You want them to be honest? Let them catch you being honest with your taxes and in every other area of your life. You want them to be patient? Be patient as you're driving.

Find other adults who demonstrate the attributes you want to see in your children, and have your kids spend time with those mentors. *Surround your children with God-honoring people, and let your kids soak it all up.*

Encourage your kids to ask questions too, especially the hard questions. I knew there was going to come a day my daughters would look at me and ask, "Dad, did you and Mom have sex before you were married?"

I was so thankful that I knew Jesus when I was dating Julie. We purposed in our hearts that we'd stay pure until we were married, so I've been able to look Yancy and Whitney in the eye and say, "Nope, but it's been great fun since our wedding." My kids know me. They know I took drugs back in the seventies. They've asked me hard questions, and I've answered them.

I've discovered that training never stops. There will be character issues to address, career developments to weigh out, and if you're lucky, discussions about people they're dating to look forward to. Encourage your kids. Catch them doing right things, and be sure to believe in your children, especially in their dreams.

I've taken some flak about how I've gone about helping both of my daughters pursue their dreams, but I want my kids and grands to pursue God's plans and purposes for their lives, not pursue my plans or purposes. So if my child wanted to be a painter, I'd take them to art shows, so they could see some good stuff, some bad stuff, and learn to know the difference. I'd expose them to the best artists so they could know the masters.

So when your daughter wants to be a rock and roller, that principle still applies. She's got to go see the masters at work. I once had my wife take our daughter to a Rolling Stones concert. You can imagine how some of the people at church responded to *that* (maybe you've got some questions too).

But can you think of a better example of longevity in rock and roll? Those guys have been around *forever*. (I keep expecting a Stones tour to be sponsored by Depend® underwear and the AARP.) The Stones have been packing out auditoriums for decades, and anyone who wants to make a life as a rock-and-roll musician can learn something by watching their showmanship and staging. Plus, there's something powerful about being next to your children when they smell marijuana for the first time at a concert. When it happens, they're with you—you're there as a safety net when they get exposed to something that can hurt them.

Are you entering into the worlds of your children and your spouse? Are you there to provide training when it's required?

7. GUARD YOUR TIME OFF.

Even Father God took a day off, but you're running around week after week without a day off. Who do you think you are?

The fact is that you need rest. And your family needs to know that if you're with them, *you're with them*. If you're streaming a game or movie and you interrupt it four times to answer your cell phone, what kind of message do you think that sends? Put that thing on silent or Do Not Disturb or better yet turn it off. Put it in another room or give all electronics a bedtime.

I let my family help me figure out what to do on my days off. It just makes sense. I want to be with them, so I might as well do things they enjoy. That policy has opened up lots of new experiences for me. For instance, I know more about designer makeup than I ever thought I'd know. And you'd be amazed at what a guy who looks like me can know about ballet too.

8. LOOK FOR MINISTRY TASKS TO DO WITH YOUR FAMILY.

Do what you can to include your family in your church work too. When my children were young, I asked them to come with me when I had to run errands for the church. One of my children helped me pick out a quarter of a million pieces of candy for a Hallelujah Night event. She thought that was way cool. What are you doing that your children could help you do? It is a fine line though. You can't force the ministry on your family.

You also don't want to penalize your children for having a parent who's a children's ministry leader. Here's what I mean: I got a call from a church worker who was getting flak about putting her own kids on stage during a children's ministry musical. I asked her, "If they weren't your kids, would they still be in the show? Are they gifted and talented in that way?"

"Absolutely," she said.

"Then don't worry about it," I told her. "Go ahead and use them."

Listen, if your kid is the right kid to sing the solo in the Christmas program, let him sing the solo. If your child has the best costume in your church's Fall Festival, give her the trophy. If people don't like it, they can lump it. Those folks can just grow up.

I don't want my children to be penalized because Daddy or Mom was called to the ministry. I want my children to cherish the call of God and recognize it as a benefit in life, not something that becomes a burden.

9. DON'T BRING PROBLEMS HOME FROM THE OFFICE.

Let your home be an oasis, a sanctuary. When you come through the door and see your kids, don't lose those first few moments of reconnecting because you're dragging home stress and anger.

My goal is to not let something that happens at work affect my attitude toward my children. Is that your goal too? Whether your kids greet you at the door with a big smile and a "Daddy's home!" or they're hunkered down in the basement streaming music on their phones and hardly know you're alive, make contact. That will be easier to do if you're not complaining about the work your pastor expects from you or about the call you got from a youth volunteer.

Make sure your spouse and children know that coming home to them is the high point of your day—that you want to enter into their worlds, not drag them into yours. I'm not suggesting you lie about how your day went. Don't pretend everything's fine if it isn't. But what will your fourteen-year-old son do about the way the church board voted on that new computer you wanted for ministry? Does griping to your son help your cause, or does it teach him to resent the church?

And here's a tip that was incredibly helpful for me. If I have to work at home, I do it in a way that lets my family know when it is okay to interrupt me. When I am tackling a job that doesn't require complete and total concentration, I work in the family room. My kids and grands wander in and out, ask me questions, tell me jokes, and tell me about their day, and that's fine. I don't get through the work quickly, but that's okay if I'm staying connected to my family. Also, I spend as little time as possible working when the kids are over.

Now, if I don't want to be interrupted, I go hide out for the minimum time necessary in my home office. That's the signal that Dad shouldn't be interrupted until later.

Consider this radical concept. If your kids are little, don't work until after your kids are in bed. They'll drift off to sleep smiling because you cuddled them, tucked them in, and prayed with them. And you usually won't have to stay up all that much later to get your work done.

10. ADMIT IT WHEN YOU MAKE MISTAKES.

If you're going to have a good family life, one of the best things you can do is be transparent. There are times when I have had to ask my family for forgiveness. I remember some years ago God showed me that I wasn't spending enough time with my family. I wasn't there for them in the way God desired and, when I slowed down and thought about it, in the way that *I* desired either. I sat them down, asked their forgiveness, and then repented. I changed my priorities and adjusted my schedule. I showed them I was sincere.

God wants you to have an excellent ministry and an excellent home life. It's not that you've got to choose one or the other. Wise leaders choose both.

CHAPTER 16:
LESSONS I'VE LEARNED THE HARD WAY

I was leading a ministry conference in Springfield, Missouri, and we had a few minutes before things got started. Rather than sit around doing nothing, I asked if anyone had questions.

A guy raised his hand and said, "Tell us about some of the mistakes you've made."

Now I knew that I'd messed up now and then, but until I started talking about it, I had no idea I'd done so many silly things.

I'm so glad there weren't video cameras when I started in children's ministry. Boy, if you could see some of the stupid stuff I did, you'd want your money back for this book, as well as, all the conference fees and webinar registrations you've paid to listen to me.

I've written about the "Great Egg Drop" (see Chapter 8). That certainly didn't go as planned. I did an egg drop again 25 years later, but it was a totally different event after I corrected every mistake I had made the first time around.

And there was the time I took a little fellow to camp who happened to be blind. I knew he was blind, but I didn't know that he'd had his eyes removed and replaced with glass lenses that could be removed like contacts. Before he got into the lake, he took his glass eyes out. *That* got the attention of the other children.

I could have gone on all day telling stories on myself, and you know what? That probably would have been fine. People like to hear about mistakes we've made, and it's not always just so they can giggle at our expense. We can learn from the mistakes of others.

When you tell me what you did that fell down or blew up or fizzled and fell flat, I can tuck that away as a lesson learned. I won't try it myself. You've spared me a painful experience.

If you're in a growing ministry, you'll find yourself doing lots of things for the first time. I remember going from a few hundred kids to thousands of kids. There were lots of times my workers looked at me when we hit a new challenge and said, "Pastor Jim, what are we going to do?" And I had to reply, "I haven't got a clue."

That's the thing about being a trailblazer. You see a lot of unfamiliar territory. When you add a new after-school program in your church, you're being a pioneer, and that means there's a lot of potential for making a mistake but also for reaching new kids. When you put new playground equipment in your side yard, you might make a mistake, but you can also bless your kids.

Here I am today after nearly fifty years still trying new things I've never done before. I'm not afraid of making mistakes because Holy Spirit is my Helper. He's a good guide that we can trust. Any time you do something that you've never done before can become a time you make a mistake, but what's the alternative? To always do what you've always done? That's fine, but there's a consequence—you'll always get what you've always gotten.

When you grow, you make mistakes; but mistakes aren't the worst thing that can happen to you. Far worse is to do nothing. And even worse than that is to make a mistake and learn nothing from it.

Anybody who is growing takes risks. Have you ever watched a child learn to walk? Mercy, it's a good thing children's little behinds are padded because they spend a lot of time landing on that padding. Very few children just stand up, dust themselves off, and take off walking.

The Wright brothers spent four years trying hundreds of times to get an airplane into the air before they figured out how to get the engineering right. They kept learning from their mistakes, taking risks, and making adjustments.

Multiple times, Abraham Lincoln ran for—and lost—elections for both the Illinois State Legislature and the US Senate before being elected President of the United States. He learned something new from each effort to run for office that got him ready for the next run. Like Lincoln, successful leaders make mistakes, and then they learn from those mistakes. It's not the mistakes that stop them; it's what they do with those mistakes.

There are times I wish I could go back to churches where I've served and do things differently. There are times I wish I could plan activities differently or say something

I didn't say. But I can't go back, and you can't either. You can only choose to go forward. And you can thank God that He's a God of second chances.

Here's some of what I've learned from my mistakes. These are things I wish I'd known when I started in ministry. I hope you'll benefit from reading these and that you'll be able to learn from my experiences.

SAY NO TO A KNOW-IT-ALL ATTITUDE.

God's Word has a lot to say to people who think they already know it all. In Proverbs 9:9 we read, "Instruct the wise and they will be wiser still; teach the righteous and they will add to their learning."

The key to being productive is to keep learning. You can learn something new every day if you want to. Make it your prayer to always be on a quest to learn what God has for you. I'll guarantee that you don't already know it all now.

If you're busy trying to convince others that you already know it all, you won't be teachable. You also won't be making any friends. Nobody comes alongside arrogant people when they trip and fall.

BUILD A TEAM. DON'T BE A ONE-PERSON SHOW.

This is a lesson I learned more than thirty years ago. When I left church number three in Alabama to move to church number four in Oklahoma, I'd trained and prepared leaders to capably direct the midweek programs, VBS, the puppet team, and Sunday school. But I'd always enjoyed leading the children's worship, so I reserved that job for my family and me.

After I'd been gone awhile, I asked some folks from that church how things were going. They told me they'd had their best VBS ever. The Sunday school was growing, and the midweek programs were booming. But when I asked about the children's worship services, he said, "I've got to be honest with you, Jim. Thanks to you, we have lousy praise and worship."

Ouch.

That had been the one area where I'd been selfish and kept doing it myself. I hadn't duplicated myself by training other people, so when I left, there was no one ready to take over. In that area of ministry, no fruit remained after I headed off to Oklahoma.

That's when I decided that no matter how much I enjoy doing some things myself, I will always prepare a successor. I'll create teams with a depth of skills and experience. I'll leave fruit that remains after I'm gone. I'm now at what I believe will be my last church assignment, church number six. I haven't made that mistake since church number three. I've chosen to be intentional to build a team.

You owe it to the people in your church to do the same thing. There's no success without a successor, and when you prepare people and release them into ministry, you release yourself, too, to do the things that only you can do.

THINK GOD'S WAY.

Philippians 4:8 says, "Finally, brothers and sisters, whatever is true, whatever is noble, whatever is right, whatever is pure, whatever is lovely, whatever is admirable—if anything is excellent or praiseworthy—think about such things."

All people in ministry should seek to know and live this verse, and let it flow from deep within their bones. Why? Because the key to a good attitude and being a leader's leader is how you think.

Don't think negatively about people. Remember the good things about your leaders, your staff, your church, and the people you serve. Focus on the positive. I'm not talking about sugarcoating anything. I know you don't have perfect people on your team. And you know what? They don't have a perfect leader. I'm not asking you to ignore the areas where people need improvement. I'm just asking you to love those people and see them as God sees them. It'll revolutionize your life and your ministry.

Do this for me. Think in steps. I know you usually hear, "Think big! Dream big! We serve a big God!" We *do* serve a big God, but He's a God of order too. And when He created the universe, He did it one step at a time. So why do you think you can jump across all the steps from here to something huge? Think small, not big. Think of how you can make one corner of your ministry excellent, and then move on to the next corner and then the next. When you get back to the first corner you fixed, you'll have learned enough to improve it even more. Then start your route over, improving things as you go.

CONSIDER OTHER PEOPLE.

When I was single and didn't have children, I used to plan things at times that made no sense for parents and families. Then I'd wonder why people didn't show up— what unspiritual people! But they weren't unspiritual. They just had a leader who didn't consider them when he set the calendar.

Who are you serving? Do you think like those people? Do you think they like the people you're discipling and training? If you don't, you'll never be effective. If there's one thing the pandemic taught us is all of our meetings don't have to be in person. You can always offer an online option. I think it's amazing when a family church makes time for family time and dares to think like busy people and families.

Think like a visitor too. You know where all the classrooms are in your building. You know where to find the bathrooms and the light switches. You know where the main auditorium is. Your visitors don't. You need to find a way to tell them with signage and a greeter or two.

LEARN FROM OTHERS.

I used to think that I had to come up with all the great ideas and solutions myself. I used to spend days reinventing the wheel.

Now when I run into a challenge, I pick up the phone and call, text, or email someone who's dealt with that problem before. People are happy to spare you the hard knocks they have experienced if you will ask for advice and be teachable.

Study people who are successful. It's easy to google others and learn from their stories. Look for models of ministry that work in situations like yours, and then borrow ideas that are helpful, but make those ideas your own. You can't expect a program that works wonderfully in Tennessee to fly in New York without some major modifications. Be willing to do that work.

COMMIT TO THE LONG HAUL.

I wish I'd been committed to the long haul earlier in my ministry. I used to be quick to give up. Things would get tough and after just a few years, I'd pack up and leave. By church number four I wanted to break this cycle, so I stopped taking things so personally and trying to handle things in my own strength, and I just worked as unto Jesus. I asked Holy Spirit to help me develop tough skin but have a tender heart. When I look back on the last thirty-plus years since I made that commitment, I'm so glad I never gave up.

It's so neat to see kids I had in children's church now fulfilling the call of God in their lives as adults. I'm glad I didn't give up and leave when things got frustrating, or I never would have seen that.

How do you do that? How do you stay put year after year?

To begin, don't let *leaving* be part of your vocabulary. My wife and I agreed when we got married that we wouldn't let divorce be an option ever. We wouldn't even use the word. We'd live by the Word of God, stay true to each other, and work through whatever came along together. We'd also let each other have a bad day sometimes. I realized that just like my wife and I allow each other to have a bad day, I had to let those I work with and serve also have a bad day every now and then.

If you're going to make a relationship with a church work long term, it takes that same sort of commitment. You've got to be willing to put your dreams on the back burner and serve others, trusting that God will take care of you and your dreams in His own timing. For almost fifty years, I've seen every dream I've ever had in ministry come true by serving others and helping them see *their* dreams come true.

A few years ago, I pulled into a gas station and was filling up the tank. A guy walked out of the station and said to me, "Jim, I want you to know you don't have to pay for your gas. I paid for it because I want to say thanks for what you're doing for my kids and family, and this is a small way to say that."

You know what that was for me? It was way more than a free tank of gas. It was a reminder that God will care for me and my family. I don't have to be afraid of failure, and I don't have to be afraid of losing my job. I can just stay here and serve God, my pastor, and the individuals and families in our ministry.

Fear is faith in reverse; perfect love casts out fear. You don't have to be afraid of failure. Just serve, and let God be your provider.

DON'T TRY TO DO EVERYTHING OVERNIGHT.

Have realistic expectations for yourself. You can't do everything. You can't do things instantly. Creating a solid, long-lasting ministry takes time.

Listen, Rome wasn't built in a day, and there were a *whole lot* of Romans working on the place. Don't be surprised if it takes you a while to build something too.

DON'T TAKE PART IN POWER PLAYS.

When I was young in ministry, I tried to get my way all the time. That approach to life doesn't work when you're a child, and it doesn't work when you're a grown-up. As children, we throw fits and demand things. We're loud and angry. Similarly, as adults we get all upset and work the angles, but then we pretend that we're really just concerned about our ministries.

Don't pout, and don't threaten. I once worked for a pastor who deserves an award for putting up with me. I'd ask for something, and when he didn't jump to do what I wanted, I'd threaten to leave. One day he'd had about all he could take of me.

"All right," he said, "go ahead and leave."

Well, I didn't want to leave, not really; I just wanted my way. It was the best thing he could have said to me. After he called my bluff, I never threatened anyone that way again.

Think about the well-being of others, of your ministry, and of your church. Be a team player. Esteem the team. Serve your leader well.

BE WILLING TO LOSE A BATTLE TO WIN A WAR.

This is a hard one because we feel like we have to defend ourselves. We just have to be right about something, so we'll fight even silly battles to make sure people know that we're right. But sometimes it's better to keep your mouth shut and not defend yourself so you don't get sucked into stupid arguments. Besides, it's God's job to defend your reputation, not yours.

I once worked on a church staff where the pastor wanted to build a certain sort of building. We'd done some research and had a proposal, but there was an architect on our board—a nice guy with good intentions—who wanted a different sort of building. He'd drawn up plans to show us what he recommended.

The pastor and I got together, and we studied the architect's drawings. We found weaknesses, some things he had in the wrong place and some things he'd forgotten to take into consideration. So I did my homework; and at the board meeting, I not only presented our idea, but I poked serious holes in the architect's work. I made him look truly dumb.

The pastor and I got what we wanted—our proposal was accepted. But when I got home, I couldn't celebrate. I'd gotten my way, but I'd done it at the expense of a godly man who was just trying to help. I felt guilty and convicted, and I deserved it.

I never should have tried to make someone else look bad, yet that's exactly what I'd done. I never should have demanded I get my way whatever the cost. So I repented, and I learned a very important lesson that I live by today—over 35 years later.

PUT YOUR FAMILY SECOND ONLY TO GOD.

If I'd known early in my ministry what I know now, I'd not have planned family vacations around ministry functions. I wouldn't have used all my time off visiting my parents and extended family.

For the first six or seven years I had children, I was still concerned about becoming a success. I worked all the time, but then it hit me. My biggest success possible was to establish a family that loves God with all its heart. And that wasn't going to happen while Daddy was taking care of everyone but the people who lived at home.

Guard your time off. Take your time off. Guard your nights. Enter into the lives of your spouse and children in intentional and caring ways. My family is my greatest sermon. I'm so thankful for my wife and our marriage, and I love spending time with my kids and now their kids! (Do you know that grandkids are the reward for not killing the first bunch?)

Build memories with your immediate family. Don't ever let your spouse and children suffer because you're in ministry.

HOW YOU PRESENT YOURSELF CONVEYS YOUR RESPECT LEVEL.

Dress appropriately. Represent your pastor well. Don't be goofy and silly.

Listen, just because you're a children's pastor doesn't mean you have to walk around with a balloon sculpture around your head every Sunday. Just because you're a youth pastor doesn't mean you need to go out and get holes drilled in your body so you can wear piercings. Don't worry about being cool.

There's *nothing* that will turn off a group of kids quicker than someone going through a midlife crisis. Kids already know they're cooler than you, so don't try to compete. If you love those kids and you're glad to see them, they'll love you back. It's really that simple.

DON'T BUILD LOYALTIES TO YOURSELF.

I wish I'd known this earlier. I used to get close to people, and then they'd leave the church. Why? Because I talked to them about things I didn't need to be talking about. I blurted out things that I should never have shared.

It's true everybody needs a best friend, but that person doesn't have to be from your church. Never confide too much in volunteers or church people. And by all means, never talk negatively about people in leadership above you.

Be your pastor's biggest fan. Make your leaders look good. Remember, you're on staff as an invited guest and as a servant. If I could change anything about how I lived out my earlier ministry life, I'd never build loyalties to myself. I'd build them only to my pastors. I'm their representative. If people can't see my leaders in me, I'm a poor representative.

IT'S NEVER TOO LATE TO LEARN.

I've had people come up to me at a conference and say, "Boy, I wish I'd heard some of these years ago." Well, me too!

The fact is that ten, twenty, thirty years ago they'd have had to find someone else to teach it to them because, many times, I didn't even know those things until the week before. I'm still learning. I have not arrived!

It's never too late to change. It's never too late to start doing ministry differently. And it's never too late to learn from the mistakes of others—including my mistakes!

God-honoring leaders care more about hearing, "Well done, good and faithful servant" than about getting a pay raise. More about being authentic than being applauded. More about servanthood than selfishness.

And always remember, leader, wake up each day knowing God has a wonderful assignment for you. That adventure may take you around the world or around the corner to buy a prop or object lesson for Sunday's sermon, but you're headed somewhere. God is leading you somewhere unique to build up His kingdom.

Ready for adventure?

Take the next step today.

Lead.

Choose to be an authentic leader.

You can do it!

—Jim Wideman

MEET JIM WIDEMAN

Throughout the past 45 years, Jim Wideman has led and guided church ministries with a clear vision of how to help leaders find solutions to seemingly impossible problems. Jim understands what priorities are important for moving the mission forward. Throughout his career, Jim has developed systems and processes to help teams make sound decisions, translate visions into action, and provide practical tools from what he's learned through personal experience. Jim is committed to not be a leader that tells people what they used to do, but to be one who tells others what he is currently doing. He is an innovated leader who has devoted his life to helping others achieve personal, spiritual, and numerical growth through consulting, training, speaking, coaching, and mentoring to churches of all sizes, denominations, and styles in America and around the world. Jim is considered one of the Fathers of the Modern Children's and Family Ministry Movement. He's served in six thriving churches as well as published 15 books, and providing coaching and consulting through Jim Wideman Ministries.

Jim's influence and innovation has been continuously acknowledged around the world. In the 1980s, The International Network of Children's Ministers (INCM) awarded him their Ministry of Excellence Award. In the 1990s, Children's Ministry magazine named him one of the Top 10 Pioneers of the Decade. In 2010, Children's Ministry magazine once again honored him by naming him one of the Top 20 Influencers in Children's Ministry. And in 2012, INCM presented Jim with their first-ever Legacy Award for his lifetime achievement in children's ministry.

Jim knows he is not yet finished. He continues to engage with and empower the next generation. Jim currently serves as the Executive Operations Pastor at The Belonging Co. in Nashville, Tennessee.

Of all the talks and teachings Jim has had the privilege of giving, He counts his family as his greatest sermon! Jim and his wife Julie, have celebrated 43 years (and counting!) of marriage and they have two grown daughters and three of the cutest grandsons you'd ever want to meet.

ALSO AVAILABLE FROM
JIM WIDEMAN

Beat The Clock
Successful Strategies for Time Management

Building Teams That Stick
Creating A Servant Reset

Connect With Your Kids
(Parenting)

Kidmin Leadership

STRETCH
Structuring Your Ministry for Growth

The Eric Trap
5 Things Every Leader Has To Get Right

Tweetable Leadership

For more information about any of these resources or for more information about
Coaching with Jim or for booking Jim to speak, check out
www.jimwideman.com

CPSIA information can be obtained
at www.ICGtesting.com
Printed in the USA
LVHW010851260921
698656LV00002B/2